KU-129-575

Cambridge Studies in Historical Geography 3

HISTORICAL UNDERSTANDING IN GEOGRAPHY

Cambridge Studies in Historical Geography

Series editors:
ALAN R. H. BAKER   J. B. HARLEY   DAVID WARD

Cambridge Studies in Historical Geography encourages exploration of the philosophies, methodologies and techniques of historical geography and publishes the results of new research within all branches of the subject. It endeavours to secure the marriage of traditional scholarship with innovative approaches to problems and to sources, aiming in this way to provide a focus for the discipline and to contribute towards its development. The series is an international forum for publication in historical geography which also promotes contact with workers in cognate disciplines.

HISTORICAL UNDERSTANDING IN GEOGRAPHY

An idealist approach

LEONARD GUELKE
Associate Professor, University of Waterloo

CAMBRIDGE UNIVERSITY PRESS
CAMBRIDGE
LONDON   NEW YORK   NEW ROCHELLE
MELBOURNE   SYDNEY

Mackland
911.2
GUE

Published by the Press Syndicate of the University of Cambridge
The Pitt Building, Trumpington Street, Cambridge CB2 1RP
32 East 57th Street, New York, NY 10022, USA
296 Beaconsfield Parade, Middle Park, Melbourne 3206, Australia

© Cambridge University Press 1982

First published 1982

Printed in Great Britain at the University Press, Cambridge

Library of Congress catalogue card number: 82-4356

British Library Cataloguing in Publication Data

Guelke, Leonard
Historical understanding in geography.
—(Cambridge studies in historical geography; 3)
1. Geography, Historical
I. Title
911   G141

ISBN 0-521-24678-4

LIVERPOOL INSTITUTE
OF HIGHER EDUCATION
THE MACKLAND LIBRARY

Accession No.
86066

Class No.
911.2 GUE

Catal.
4 . 5 . 86 AE

BO

FOR JANET

Contents

Preface

Although many geographers have used historical approaches in the study of human activity, the historical approach as such has not been widely viewed as a fundamental mode of geographical understanding. The lack of interest in historical analysis conceived of as a mode of understanding is partly the result of the social scientific, generalizing, and anti-idiographic orientation of much modern geography. Yet even before the triumph of a social scientific view of their discipline, many geographers, notwithstanding their sympathies with the idea that geographers studied unique regions, defined their discipline in a way that left little room for any kind of historical analysis. The pedestrian character of much human geography in the man–land and regional traditions was in large measure due to its lack of a historical dimension. In failing to appreciate the potential importance of historical understanding in human geography, geographers deprived themselves of a philosophical justification of the traditional man–land and regional approach, and missed an opportunity of adding intellectual depth to such studies.

This work puts forward a case for historical geography conceived of both as a field in its own right and as the foundation of a revitalized traditional, empirical human geography. The crux of the case rests on the proposition that historical enquiry is an independent form of understanding, not based upon or related to the approaches of the natural or social sciences. In recognizing history as an independent form of knowledge one is able to look at historical geography from a new perspective.

The approach to historical understanding advanced here is based upon Oxford philosopher and historian R. G. Collingwood's posthumously published book *The idea of history* (1946). Although Collingwood was a brilliant and independent thinker, his ideas on history did not develop in a vacuum of ideas. The eighteenth century philosopher Vico, Kant, Hegel, the German neo-Kantian Rickert, the idealist Bradley, Dilthey, the Italian philosopher Croce and the Cambridge scholar Michael Oakeshott, among others, all contributed important ideas to Collingwood's position. Yet Collingwood's views do not rest on the authority of those who influenced him. In *The idea of history* he presented a major logical defense of an idealist approach to history that must be assessed on its merits.

This book seeks to develop some implications of an idealist approach to historical understanding for geography. The position I present must be assessed as a whole in relation to its assumptions and the logic of the arguments advanced in its defense. The validity of my case would not have been strengthened by attempting to buttress it with a 'scissors and paste' collection of quotations from scholars who might have said similar things in different contexts. Where quotations are used they have largely been drawn from Collingwood or his interpreters. These quotations must themselves be assessed in terms of the contribution they make to my overall argument, rather than being construed as appeals to authority. If I have had an overriding concern it has been to present a logical, self-contained and coherent account of the nature of historical understanding in geography.

A number of people read and commented on the manuscript. I am indebted to Fraser Hart, Peter Nash, Richard Preston, Robert Shell and George Sitwell all of whom read the entire manuscript and made valuable suggestions for its improvement. Fraser Hart deserves a special mention for the great care he took in his comments. A summer school engagement at the University of British Columbia provided an opportunity for a number of productive discussions with Graeme Wynn and Cole Harris. My thinking has also benefited from the contributions of Helen Couclelis, Michael Curry, Christian Dufournaud, Inez Egerbladh and Richard Elphick. The series editors, Alan Baker and Brian Harley, had many constructive ideas about how the manuscript could be strengthened. For all this help, I am most grateful.

Especial thanks go to Joan MacLean of the University of Waterloo who skillfully typed the original manuscript and cheerfully made all the changes that were necessary as a result of major revisions.

Needless to say, the views expressed in this work are not necessarily shared by those I have mentioned, and remain entirely my responsibility.

Portions of Chapters 2 and 5 of this study have appeared in the author's 'An idealist alternative in human geography', *Annals of the Association of American Geographers,* **64** (1974), 193–202 (Chapter 2) and 'Frontiers settlement in early Dutch South Africa', *Annals of the Association of American Geographers* **66** (1976), 25–42 (Chapter 5). I wish to thank the Executive Director of the Association of American Geographers for permission to use material from these articles.

Introduction

This work is based upon the contention that history is an autonomous field of knowledge, quite distinct from the natural and social sciences, with objectives, concepts and procedures of its own. The term 'history' is used here in its broadest meaning to include all the disciplines concerned with approaching or understanding human societies as historical creations. History is seen as the fundamental foundation of human studies. What theory is to the natural sciences, history is to the study of human society. The autonomy of history is not a question relating to the current status of knowledge in the field, but is absolutely basic and a logical consequence of its objectives and subject matter.

History is the study of the world humans have made for themselves. The human species is the only species that has created its own society. The historical study of human society is concerned with that creation as a human invention. On this view, history is by definition restricted to the study of human society. This is not to deny the existence of other kinds of studies of the past, but those studies are not considered 'history'. The study of past states of the natural world, for example, falls within the domain of the appropriate specialized discipline. Although such studies might be referred to as (natural) history, the idea of history as this word is used in relation to human society cannot by the very nature of things exist. The natural world did not create itself and its study can be successfully pursued using standard scientific procedures.

The essence of the position presented here is conveyed, in Collingwood's words, by the sentence 'All history is the history of thought.' This statement, which has come in for much criticism, far from being an overstatement, provides the essential foundation of history conceived of as an independent form of knowledge. The idea that all history necessarily involves thought should not be seen as an absurd claim concerning the independence of mind from physical, biological and psychological forces, but as a recognition that the historical significance of such forces is dependent on and defined by the human mind. The historian is not interested in natural and social phenomena as phenomena, but in the way they are construed in specific social contexts.

1

History is by definition limited to the mind, and the mind cannot comprehend the real world directly. In proclaiming that history is the province of mind, one makes a clean and total break with positivism. History is no longer concerned with explanation (in the natural-scientific sense of initial conditions and laws) but with understanding events and actions in terms of the thought expressed in them.

The historical scholar is in a privileged position for studying human society because he is himself a member of it. This relationship of the investigator to his subject matter has no parallel in the natural sciences. The natural scientist must always be an outside observer, he can never obtain an inside view. Although a historian is not able to see directly into the minds of his subjects, he is able to understand their actions as being products, like his, of rational thought. The actions of the past can be understood by the historian re-enacting in his own mind the thought in them. This process of re-enactment or *re-thinking* is the foundation of all historical fields concerned with human society.

The concept of understanding in terms of re-enactment of thought is not the equivalent of a natural scientific explanation. The historian, in re-thinking the thought in an action, seeks to make sense of it, seeks to make it intelligible. Understanding is achieved when the scholar is able to comprehend an action as the expression of the thought of the individual or group under investigation. This procedure should not be thought of as requiring empathetic understanding in an emotional sense. Although the ability to see things from the points of view of people of different cultures and periods does require imagination, the imagination must be disciplined and historical inferences must conform to the available evidence.

In traditional philosophical terms the position presented here can be classified under the broad heading of idealism. The philosophy of idealism recognizes mind as the foundation of human existence and knowledge. For the idealist, in contrast to the realist, what is known is not independent of the knower. This principle finds expression in the idea that history can be conceived of as a process of thought. Although the term 'idealist' is a useful way to distinguish this approach to historical understanding from those of the realist and materialist, the philosophy of idealism encompasses a wide range of philosophical ideas. In the final analysis, no broad heading can adequately convey the nature of a specific philosophical position, which defines itself as it is developed.

There is a need for historical understanding in geography, because human activity on the land is a product of historical experience. In creating his own society and culture, man also produced new forms of geographical life. A basic task of historical geography is to understand the nature of these forms of life by investigating the ideas on which they are based. Although an important aspect of such an investigation will involve an analysis of environmental ideas and geographical knowledge, the historical geographer will be as much, if not more, concerned with social, economic and political ideas expressed in human actions on the earth. This task involves probing the geographical implications of the unique historical experiences of the earth's peoples.

The historical approach ultimately makes a contribution to an understanding of the present by elucidating the geographical ramifications of historical change. This does not mean that historical geographical work need always terminate with the present, but it does mean that the study of present is scarcely conceivable within a nonhistorical framework. The historical approach is seen as providing the foundation of regional geography conceived of as a quest for an intellectual understanding of human forms of life.

The central role of historical analysis in all human geography makes it possible to claim that 'all geography is historical geography'. This statement, however, should not be misconstrued. In the context of the position advocated here, it means that human geography studies human activity on the land conceived of as a creation of human ideas. All geography is historical geography only in so far as it focuses on the evolution of human thought and its geographical expressions. This position leaves no place for human or historical geography conceived of as an external spectacle. This does not exclude such things as ecological studies from geography, but merely classifies such work as belonging to the physical or natural science branch of the discipline. The fundamental divide is not between human and physical geography as such, but rather between those aspects of human activity that are a reflection of mind (ideas) and those that are not.

Historical geography is considered to be just one of many historical fields, differentiated only by its focus on human geographical topics from other fields of history. The historical geographer is mainly concerned with human activity on the surface of the earth, but his interest in the past encompasses any phenomenon which might in some way have a bearing on such activities. The validity of this concept of history is not affected by the nature of the (human) topics of interest to historical geographers. Historical geography can in fact be defined as the study of changes in thought expressed in human activity on the surface of the earth. This definition has the potential of providing a foundation for a stronger and more coherent field. The idea that historical geography encompasses the entire geographic past is inadequate because it provides no criterion of historical geographical significance. Historical geography has already, in the absence of a clear idea of history, become a series of independent endeavours with few common threads.

The organization of this work reflects a desire to establish historical geography as a legitimate field of historical knowledge. In Chapter 1, I argue that a limiting concept of history has been widely accepted by historical geographers. History is not a synonym for the past. Historians and historical geographers are concerned, first and foremost, with the historical meaning of the past. The widely diffused (often implicit) positivist or natural-scientific notions that the historian is concerned with phenomena of the past as events whose causes are to be discovered, must be replaced by a concern with elucidating their historical meaning in terms of human thought and action.

The idea of re-thinking is considered in Chapters 2 and 3. The meaning of the world is a function of ideas. To understand a historical situation and the actions that are part of it, one must reconstruct and re-think the thoughts of those involved, because it is these thoughts that give meaning to human actions. In Chapter 2 re-thinking is put forward as the foundation upon which historical knowledge rests, and, in Chapter 3, I defend the concept against objections that have been raised against it.

In Chapter 4, I place the idealist approach in a wider context, and some problems of a positivist and Marxist history are considered. The positivist approach to history is premised on the use of laws which are wanting and no adequate criteria are presented on which historical phenomena can be differentiated from other past phenomena. Although there is a strong historical component in Marxian analysis, the approach is judged wanting, because Marxists have failed to indicate how their theoretical propositions might be adequately tested in empirical contexts.

Chapter 5 is an illustration of an idealist historical approach. The illustration is a study of the transformation of the early Dutch settlement of South Africa. In it an attempt is made to explain the development of settlement as a dialectical process involving the logical development of ideas.

Chapter 6 seeks to bring together some of the main points I have attempted to establish in the preceding chapters, and to elaborate on some of the ways in which traditional empirical human geography might be revitalized on the foundations of historical geography.

1

Inadequate concepts of history in Historical Geography

The word 'history' is not considered a synonym for the past, nor even the human past. The historian has always been at pains to differentiate himself from the chronicler and antiquarian, both of whom have an interest in the human past. The concept of history implies more than a mere ordering of past events, which is the task of the chronicler. It also implies something different from the kinds of analyses conducted within the social sciences. A fundamental concern of the historian is to evaluate the significance of past actions. This idea of evaluation and selection is clearly indicated in the words 'historic event'. Not all past events or actions are of historic interest; indeed the terms 'historic event' and 'historic action' imply the existence of criteria on the basis of which certain events or actions are separable from others in terms of their inherent historical importance.

The basis on which a human action or event acquires historical status is a crucial question in the philosophy of history. No historian is able to re-create the past as it actually happened; every history involves a selection of facts. Yet this selection must be based on criteria of what constitutes historical importance if the word 'history' is to have a meaning beyond a synonym for things that happened in the past. Even if the actual criteria on which phenomena acquire historical status are not always clear, the existence of such criteria is not in doubt. Indeed, if criteria of selection were not available there would be no logical basis for saying that one account of the past was better than another (provided each contained factual statements).

At this point, I will not elaborate in more detail on the idea of history. It is sufficient that the reader accept that a scholar concerned with the past cannot re-create or reconstruct the past as it actually was, but, of necessity, creates an account of it based upon a selection of facts. The basis on which a historian selects his facts is the crucial characteristic that differentiates him from other scholars that are also concerned with the past. This idea of history has not found strong expression in geography.

The concepts of historical geography which are widely accepted by modern

5

geographers are based upon partially developed ideas about the meaning of history. This situation is largely the outgrowth of the particular circumstances surrounding the development of academic historical geography, and must itself be understood historically. The ideas about historical geography that were developed by such leading figures as Hartshorne, Sauer, Darby, and Clark were based upon a temporal concept of history. This concept of history has been widely accepted by historical geographers, including many scholars, such as Wright, with humanist persuasions. Historical geographers can strengthen and add definition to their field by making an explicit concept of history an integral part of it.

The problem of the idea of history in historical geography is partly related to the tradition of philosophical and methodological discussion in geography. Geographers have been inclined to consider philosophical and methodological questions in isolation from other disciplines. Harvey decisively broke with this tradition in *Explanation in geography*, but, as yet, historical geographers have given little indication of recognizing that the extensive literature in the philosophy of history is of vital importance to them.[1] When modern ideas or new concepts about history are put forward the references are to geographers, sociologists and anthropologists rather than philosophers of history. Where attempts have been made to introduce historical geographers to work of a philosophical character, that work has often been marginally historical in content.[3]

Even in cases where historical geographers have shown awareness of stronger concepts of history, this knowledge has not usually been properly integrated into their concept of historical geography.[4] The mere affirmation of an idea is considered of no real importance until that idea is made a vital part of an individual's overall position on a given topic. In an intellectual sense, an idea is only of importance where it can be *logically* integrated within a coherent set of ideas. On this basis it is argued that historical geographers have lacked an adequate concept of history.

Hartshorne, Sauer, Darby, and Clark

Although Hartshorne's specific position on historical geography has never been widely accepted by historical geographers, his basic ideas have been of considerable importance in channelling thinking about historical geography along certain lines. In *The nature of geography* Hartshorne enlisted the support of the philosopher Immanuel Kant in seeking to find a logical place for geography among the sciences. Hartshorne referred to the views of Kant (presented as an introduction to lectures on physical geography) as follows:

The point of view there developed has proved so satisfactory, to others as well as to this writer, both in leading to an understanding of the nature of geography and in providing answers to all questions that have been raised, that it seems worth while to quote at some length from Kant's original statements.[5]

The essence of Kant's position (as it was interpreted by Hartshorne, and I am not concerned here with the historical accuracy of this interpretation) was the distinction it drew between the logical classification of perceptions according to concepts and the physical one according to space and time. Hartshorne, quoting Kant, wrote:

Description according to time is history, that according to space is geography. . . . History differs from geography only in the consideration of time and area (*Raum*). The former is a report of phenomena that follow one another (*nacheinander*) and has reference to time. The latter is a report of phenomena beside each other (*nebeneinander*) in space. History is narrative, geography a description. . . . Geography and history fill up the entire circumference of our perceptions: geography that of space, history that of time.[6]

On these premises Hartshorne, a consistent and logical thinker, correctly concluded that a narrative historical geography was impossible. This conclusion was clearly stated by himself in a later work.

In the sense of 'history' as the description of variation through time and of geography as variation through space, the two could not be combined – in this sense there would be no place for 'historical geography'.[7]

In *The nature of geography*, therefore, Hartshorne held that the only legitimate type of historical geography was the geography of a temporal cross-section, that is a geography dealing with the historic present of an area or region.

Although Hartshorne had differentiated history and geography on logical grounds, his final argument for keeping the two fields separate was pragmatic. He wrote:

Theoretically one might construct an unlimited number of separate historical geographies of any region, and if these could be compared in rapid succession one would have a motion picture of the geography of an area from the earliest times to the present. In practice however this is utterly impossible – hence indeed the separation of history and geography.[8]

The concept of historical geography as a cross-section through time has been adopted in a number of historical geographical studies.[9] The objective of such studies was to provide a detailed account of the geography of the study area for the historic present. In principle, cross-sectional studies are no different from geographies of modern authors. Although the cross-section involves a study of the past, it lacks the vital element of historical development, or change through time. Narrative is one of the central concepts of almost all ideas of history, and a cross-section is concerned with the description of an area at a particular time. Although such works often contain some historical narrative, narrative is not central to the idea of a cross-section. If one grants historical status to such studies one must conclude that all geography is historical geography (where historical is used as a synonym for past or of the past), and the only difference between a historical study and a nonhistorical one is a question of degree. Hartshorne recognized this problem in suggesting that there was 'no place for historical geography' in geography. In other words, he considered the study of past cross-sections a valid kind of geography but denied that it really qualified to be designated 'historical'. The essentially nonhistorical character of cross-sectional historical geography, however, has not been so thoroughly appreciated by other geographers, many of whom consider the cross-section a legitimate (if somewhat limiting) approach to the study of historical geography.

The view Hartshorne presented in *The nature of geography* was criticized by many historical geographers, because it was seen to promote far too limited a concept of the field. Hartshorne later revised somewhat his earlier rigid position on historical geography. In *Perspective on the nature of geography*, he conceded that a geographer might combine historical and geographical approaches (according to Hartshorne's conception of them), but he established criteria for differentiating historical and geographical work in keeping with his earlier views. He argued:

> If the concern is to determine the manner and process of change, the study may be considered essentially historical in character, if focused on the changing character and relationships of a feature considered as part of the total geography of the area, its geographic character is clear.[10]

Hartshorne used an analogy of a motion picture which he argued would obviously be geographic if each of the individual photographs was.

Although some concessions were made to historical geographical practice, the basic foundation of Hartshorne's ideas about historical geography were much the same in *Perspective on the nature of geography* as they had been in *The nature of geography*. The conception of history underlying Hartshorne's ideas, had severe weaknesses. First, for Hartshorne, history was synonymous with past time; he did not differentiate between the past as such and the historic past. Second, Hartshorne's concept of history was not limited to human history – he made no distinction between changes due to natural processes and those due to human activity. This shortcoming was the more surprising because he was at pains to emphasize that geographers study 'the earth as the home of man'. Third, it is clear from the examples Hartshorne cited that history was conceived of as a process of change in the external appearance of things. The idea that a motion picture could capture historical change is particularly illuminating of his view on this question.

Sauer put forward an important alternative idea of historical geography in which he firmly rejected Hartshorne's concept of the field.[11] Sauer considered historical geography to be an integral part of human geography which was conceived of as the study of the cultural landscape. The specific geographic expressions of culture were such things as fields, pastures, woods, mines, roads, homes and workshops.)The geographer could not, Sauer argued, study such things without asking himself about their origins. Thus, for Sauer, historical geography was in essence the analysis of geographical processes, and was of necessity concerned with origins and change.[12]

The main emphasis of Sauer's historical geography was on changes in the landscape. He was particularly concerned with the environmental consequences of human activity, much less concerned with human society as such. The foundation of Sauer's historical geography was the geographical expression of culture, not culture change itself. Exactly why cultures stagnated or changed often seemed less important than measuring their geographical expressions, where possible in the field. Thus Sauer was prompted to ask a question such as: 'Were Virginians great colonizers because they were notable soil wasters?'[13] not, 'Why were Virginians great soil wasters?' still less, 'What historical conditions created Virginian farming methods?'

Although Sauer was able to free himself from the essentially nonhistorical geography of Hartshorne, his own concept of history was poorly developed. In fact Sauer has little to say about history as such, apart from noting that human geography, unlike psychology and history, had nothing to do with individuals but only with institutions and cultures.[14] Sauer's central notion of process owed more to natural science than it did to history, notwithstanding his rejection of laws of human geography. A few remarks about the importance of being able 'to see the land with the eyes of its former occupants, from the standpoint of their needs and capacities' were not developed into anything that could be construed as a philosophy of history.[15] When it came to selecting topics for historical geographical research most of Sauer's proposals could be accommodated within the theme of man's impact on Nature.

The lack of an adequate concept of history was of no real consequence for Sauer, because he focused on problems that treated man as part of Nature. Indeed, to understand the ecological consequences of human activity, it is not necessary for the historical geographer to deal with man as an intellectual being. Such historical geography is, in fact, often entirely within the realm of the natural sciences, and requires no special methods. The ecological orientation of Sauer and many of his students made their temporal concept of history and their process-based view of change entirely suitable for many of their purposes, but it placed definite limits on the kinds of questions historical geographers could effectively address.

Darby's position on the nature of historical geography has elements in common with the ideas of both Hartshorne and Sauer. Darby, like Sauer, was not prepared to restrict historical geographical analysis to the reconstruction of period geographies. In connection with such studies he rightly noted that they were open to criticism 'because they lacked a historical approach'.[16] Nevertheless, Darby argued that the method of successive cross-sections had much to recommend it, in spite of certain practical difficulties associated with the method. The fact that (at least in theory) Darby could envisage a series of cross-sections as comprising the historical element in historical geography suggests that he identified history with change and the passage of time.

In spite of his reservations about period reconstructions, Darby put forward a theoretical justification of historical geography that is remarkably close to that of Hartshorne. Thus, Darby wrote:

> The continuity of the present-day is but a thin layer that even at this moment is becoming history. . . . Can we draw a line between geography and history? The answer is 'no', for the process of becoming is one process. All geography is historical geography, either actual or potential.[17]

The above thought was amplified using the same analogy that Hartshorne had adopted in seeking to clarify the nature of historical geography. Darby argued:

> The landscape we see is not a static arrangement of objects. It has become what it is, and it is usually in the process of becoming something different. A close analogy is to regard our momentary glimpse of it as a 'still' taken out of a long film.[18]

Darby, however, drew a somewhat different conclusion than Hartshorne did from the above analogy. He continued: 'Let us then not study a static picture, but a process that is continuing and, seemingly, never-ending'.[19]

Thus, although Darby shared many of the basic assumptions of Hartshorne about the nature of geography and history, his final position on the need to investigate process is similar to Sauer's. This similarity is also manifest in the list of themes that Darby identified as appropriate for analysis by process-oriented historical geographers. These themes, which are sometimes referred to as 'vertical' themes, included, among others: the clearing of the wood, the draining of the marsh, the reclamation of the heath lands and changes in settlement.

There was a strong element of what might be termed 'common sense' in Darby's view of historical geography; he was prepared to recognize the advantages of different approaches in historical geography.[20] On a more philosophical level Darby is open to the criticisms that have already been levelled at Hartshorne. The idea that history is essentially a selection of past events integrated into a logical narrative was not developed. All events in the past seemed to qualify as history.[21] Darby made no distinction between the natural past and the human past, and no special methods of study were presented for the study of change in the world of man. For Darby, as for Hartshorne and to a lesser extent for Sauer, historical geography was basically a spectacle of external changes in the form of things.

Clark put forward a concept of historical geography which owed much to both Sauer and Hartshorne. Clark accepted from Sauer the idea that geographers must be concerned with process and change, but sought to place this idea within a Hartshornian framework. Accepting the basic Hartshornian notions that geography was concerned with space and history with time, Clark conceived of historical geography as a kind of interdisciplinary field in which both time and space were important.[22] The historical geographer was distinguished from the historian by his greater emphasis on spatial relations, but Clark emphasized that it would not be profitable to draw a sharp demarcation line between the two disciplines. These basic ideas were summed up in Clark's characterization of historical geography as the study of 'geographical change through time'.[23] This position had many similarities to the 'vertical theme' of Darby.

Clark worked out his ideas on historical geography at a time when geographers were preoccupied with questions of approach and methods, and he failed to appreciate the weaknesses inherent in his temporal concept of history. In comparing geography and history he noted that historical geography was similar to history in giving 'attention to differentiation through time'.[24] Although Clark also identified the discipline of history 'to mean that discipline which is concerned primarily with human society in its various facets',[25] he did not restrict his idea of history in historical geography to human society. In discussing the scope of historical geography Clark wrote:

Any study of past geography or geographical change through time is historical geography, whether the study be involved with cultural, physical, or biotic phenomena and however limited it may be in topic or area. Historical geography, therefore, is like regional geography in that its concepts and methods are applicable to all branches of the subject.[26]

For Clark there was no logical distinction between natural history and human history, and a historical geographer had a licence 'to go back in time as far as he has interest and competence'.[27]

The idea of a single past, of a history embracing the natural and human worlds, was entirely consistent with Clark's Berkeley legacy which treated man as an integral part of Nature. Indeed, this theme was underlined in Clark's first major work, which carried the title *The invasion of New Zealand by people, plants and animals* (1948). In view of this natural history conception of history, it was not surprising that Clark paid little attention to the meaning of history which, for Clark, was synonymous with process and change and questions relating to the historicity of events scarcely arose. Even less was Clark concerned with deeper philosophical issues pertaining to the character of historical knowing.

Historical geography and the concept of history

The temporal concept of history found in the writings of Hartshorne, Sauer, Darby and Clark was widely accepted in historical geography. Historical geographers did not, of course, imagine that they could reconstruct the 'real' past. They recognized that every historical geographical study involved a selection of facts and that such selection would be based on certain criteria established, implicitly or explicitly, by the historical geographer, but the temporal concept failed to provide historical geographers with any explicitly historical criteria on which to make their selection. In brief, historical geography was treated no differently from historical geology, but for the geologist the history of rocks is a process of external changes in the form of things – it cannot be anything else. The history of human activity treated along the same lines simply fails to recognize that internal relationships, rather than external ones, provide the key to understanding human societies.

The discipline of history is restricted to the study of human affairs, because historians have implicitly recognized a fundamental distinction between the study of Nature and human society. Collingwood has identified the basis of this distinction.

A natural process is a process of events, an historical process is a process of thoughts. Man is regarded as the only subject of historical process, because man is regarded as the only animal that thinks, or thinks enough and clearly enough, to render his actions the expressions of his thoughts.[28]

The widespread idea that history is synonymous with the past was detrimental to historical geographical investigations in that it encouraged scholars to see human activity as a spectacle rather than as a historical creation. A number of concepts like culture and culture traits permitted historical geographers to gloss over the basic differences between the human and natural worlds. Yet the use of such concepts often meant that important historical questions were never asked. For example, the idea that ethnic groups could provide a foundation on which the historical geography of a region might be elucidated, assumes that an ethnic group exists outside the historical process 'so to speak' instead of being created (and destroyed) by it. A major weakness of Clark's *Three centuries and the island* was that it lacked a clear sense of history.[29]

The investigation of past human actions on the land has the potential of being a fully historical field. This potential can be realized if historical geographers focus their attention on the meaning of human actions of geographical interest, not merely their geographical expressions. In this context the word 'historical' does not refer to the 'discipline of history', but it is used to distinguish ideas and actions that help us understand how human activity on the land has developed from those that do not. A conscious effort is needed to relate geographical activity to the social and institutional complexes within which it is imbedded. In other words, geographers must ask questions like 'What historical conditions created Virginian farming methods?' if they are going to understand the meaning of the geographical expressions of these methods. An explicitly historical, historical geography would not be concerned with geographical change *per se*, but rather with historical changes of geographical significance.

A feeling that much historical geographical writing lacked analytical depth led some to conclude that historical geography might be strengthened by the adoption of a more explicitly scientific approach using theories and models developed in other branches of the discipline.[30] The adoption of such an approach, that is, an explicitly theoretical or model-oriented approach, would not strengthen historical geography but eliminate it entirely. The study of, for example, the centrality of fifteenth-century Moscow or the central places of eighteenth-century France is no different to modern studies of such phenomena. The past becomes a huge reservoir of data akin to the laboratory of the chemist for testing theoretical propositions and models. This past is simply not a historical past. These kinds of studies, although not history, might comprise valuable additions to the literature of theoretical geography.

The idea of history as applied social science is also inadequate for much the same reasons. The social sciences each have their own categories of analysis, which are generally independent of specific historical conditions. Yet it is the essential task of the historical scholar to explicate the meaning of activity in its historical context. A full-scale interdisciplinary study of a specific area or period might provide an enormous amount of detail about a society of the past, but such detail will not become historically meaningful unless it is related to the logical process of the human self-development of mind. In the absence of a concept of history or any credible overarching theory the study of the past becomes an accumulation of historically unconnected case studies.[31]

The social-scientific view of history is taken to its logical and unworkable theoretical conclusion in the idea of 'total' history.[32] There is no such thing as total history. Rather, there are an unlimited number of specific histories. In each specific history the focus is on changes that are historically significant for that particular topic. There is no question of restricting the evidence that might be relevant to a particular theme, but any evidence that is presented must be assessed from a specific historical point of view. In a historical geographical enquiry the character of a settlement might be attributed to economic, demographic and political factors. The historical geographer's task is to analyse the contribution of these elements by elucidating their historical meanings in the special circumstances under investigation.

The essence of history is a distinctive point of view; and history conceived of as a process of thought is quite separate both from the natural and social sciences. Although it might be quite possible to incorporate the results of a sociological or anthropological study of the past into a historical narrative, a sociological or anthropological study of the past is not history. The local (historical) study that does not deal with questions relating to the transformation of society has no historical status as such. There is danger that local studies of the past conducted within a social science paradigm will retard rather than advance historical understanding, because there is no overall integrating conception of historical process.

Alternative ideas   METHODOLOGICAL APPROACH.

Although much historical geographical scholarship can still be categorized as 'positivist', the past decade has witnessed a growing interest in, and awareness of, alternative approaches in geography.[33] This development, particularly in its philosophical emphasis, is a new departure in historical geography, but it is not without historical roots. An early proponent of an alternative 'humanist' approach to historical geography that drew inspiration from the discipline of history rather than the natural and social sciences was John K. Wright.[34] Although Wright's work was widely respected in geography, he did not hold a university position and lacked an opportunity of exercising a more direct influence on students of historical geography. Nevertheless, Wright was able in his writings to present a model of historical geography grounded in a historical–literary tradition of scholarship.

Wright exercised a major influence on geography in emphasizing that each society had its own distinctive geographical ideas and that a major task of geography involved understanding the earth from the points of view of its inhabitants. Wright coined the word 'geosophy' to denote this concept and he defined it as:

the study of geographical knowledge from any or all points of view . . . it covers the geographical ideas, both true and false, of all manner of people – not only geographers, but farmers and fishermen, business executives and poets, novelists and painters, Bedouins and Hottentots – and for this reason it necessarily has to do in large degree with subjective conceptions.[35]

The concept of geosophy was an invitation to geographical intellectual history and a number of historical geographers, notably Glacken and Tuan, took up the theme in a variety of contexts.[36]

The emergence of behavioural and perception geography as a major research theme in modern geography was an explicit recognition of the importance of understanding human behaviour in relation to subjective conceptions of the earth. However, much of the research in this area was conducted within an explicitly social-scientific paradigm, oriented to the needs of theoretical rather than historical geography.[37] Within historical geography environmental ideas were investigated and used in the explanation of human exploration and settlement behaviour, but this interest in the subjectivity of perception was not developed into a philosophical position. Billinge, in an exploration of phenomenology and historical geography, concluded:

the interest shown in the reconstruction of perceived environments can be seen as a pragmatic solution to a long-standing problem, not the result of a serious change in underlying philosophy. This is particularly evident once one examines substantive examples; for though the idea of subjectivity is often incorporated, the actual technique of reconstruction often remains positivist – a-priori assumptions are not 'bracketed out' and an objective 'scientific' method is still adopted with respect to the abstraction of material and the logic of analysis.[38]

The positivist orientation of modern behavioural and perception geography meant that historical geographers adopting these approaches were not stimulated into questioning the widely accepted temporal concept of history.

If Wright's concept of geography was not preserved in the development of behavioural and perception studies, many historical geographers remained committed to a 'humanistic' view of historical geography. In the 1970s this concept was restated in a more explicit and philosophical way. Harris argued for a broadly based historical geography and emphasized the crucial role of synthesis in historical geographical enquiry.[39] He gives specific attention to the historian's problem of selection. He wrote:

No one can pack into any study the vast array of relevant data that survive from the past; were this possible the data would simply be transferred from one depository to another. Invariably a selection is made. A document is read, a short note is taken, the document is returned to its archival folder, and the note, one of thousands of selections from the data in any major study, is returned to a card file. But on what basis is this selection made, when research procedures cannot be standardized and interpretation cannot be deduced from overarching covering laws? In this predicament there is probably no alternative to a scholar's considered and informed judgement.[40]

Harris elaborated on this concept of judgement, and indicated that it was not independent of the background of a scholar but could not be equated with personal whim or opinion, because a historical interpretation can only be entertained when it 'fits the facts'.

Although Harris identified the central importance of judgement in historical geography, he failed to establish an objective basis for that judgement. In the absence of a clear concept of history, no logical grounds would exist for preferring one study of the past from another, provided both accorded with the facts. In addition to any other ideas a historian may bring with him to the study of the past, he must above all have a clear concept of history itself. Historians do criticize each other's interpretations and such criticism must, if it is to lead to a genuine dialogue, be based upon some general principles of historical selection. Such principles provide a basis on which a historian's judgement can be criticized in an objective way, that is, it can be criticized for failing to meet certain general requirements that any historical account must meet.

In other words, the idea of judgement must be related to a specific concept of history – if limits are to be placed on subjectivity in the choice of material for inclusion in a historical narrative. The boundaries of historical enquiry must be made explicit and historical judgement exercised in relation to them. Otherwise a historian would be in the position of an umpire who was called upon to officiate at a tennis match to be played on a court without lines or net. The calls made by such an umpire would require judgement, but the judgement would not be based on any objectively established limits. History must be pursued on an objective foundation, if a historian is to be properly accountable for the judgements he makes about what he chooses to put into his narrative.

In discussing the nature of historical geography, Harris questioned the idea that history and geography could be defined in terms of time and space respectively, but he nevertheless retained an essentially temporal concept of history.[41] Collingwood's idea that 'all history is the history of thought' was rejected as defining too narrowly the nature of history.[42] The identification of history with thought provides a criterion of historical significance that a temporal concept lacks, and is the central foundation of Collingwood's idealist view of history.

Billinge has explored the relevance of phenomenology in historical geography, and suggests that idealism can be conceived of as an essentially phenomenological approach.[43] Although there are similarities between phenomenological and idealist ideas, the idealist philosophies of scholars like Croce and Collingwood were developed explicitly in relation to problems of historical knowledge. It seems a retrogressive step to explore philosophical alternatives in which history as a field of knowledge does not get any special consideration. Not surprisingly, questions relating to the concept of history which receive explicit attention from philosophers of history, such as the problem of selection, are not even raised by Billinge.

Ernst and Merrens also sought to provide a basis on which historical geography could establish a satisfactory existence.[44] They argued that meaning is central to understanding reality, which clearly implies a human context of assessment, not a natural-scientific one. Yet Ernst and Merrens failed to develop this idea of meaning in a historical context. Historical geographers are not concerned with meaning as such but with historical meaning. What criteria can be used by the historical geographer in deciding which events or actions are historically meaningful? This is the central issue of historical knowing in historical geography as much as it is in any other historical field.

The shortcomings of positivist approaches in human geography have been dealt with in greater depth by Gregory.[45] However, Gregory found it easier to identify the problems of the positivist approach than he did to put forward an alternative that is not itself open to serious criticism. Gregory relied heavily on anthropological and sociological sources in the construction of an alternative historical geography, and failed to do justice to the special problems of historical enquiry.[46] Where Gregory made stronger contact with historical issues, he based much of his position on a rigid structuralism, which is subject to the same criticisms that can be made against positivist theoretical history, namely that it creates order at the expense of empirical reality.[47]

Moodie and Lehr came closer to identifying a satisfactory meaning for the word 'historical' in historical geography. They pointed out that the past is not synonymous with the historic past, and that the mere passage of time does not make contemporary geography historical geography, but, rather, makes it old geography.[48] They did not identify properly the distinctiveness of the historian's point of view, however, and fell back on the notion of facts becoming historical in relation to theories. They did not recognize any differences between natural history and human history, and all the criticisms set out above can be applied to their position.

The lack of a clear focus in historical geography is nicely illustrated by Prince, who, in looking at work within historical geography, classified it on the basis of whether a scholar was concerned with the real, the perceived, or the abstract.[49] This classification was made possible because of the lack of integration of historical geography. There were scholars like Darby and Clark who were mainly involved in the reconstruction of past geographies; some, like Wright, moved from perception studies to intellectual history and, more recently, others have used abstract theoretical approaches. The idealist approach to history provides a basis for a more coherent historical geography. Such an approach would entail a marriage of the real and the perceived, and elimination of the abstract. The perceived world – or rather the world view of individuals – is reflected in actions. The essential task of historical analysis is to show how external change is related to the development of thought. There is no question of denying the existence of the real world and every available technique will be used to establish what happened in a physical sense. The historical meanings of external actions, however, must be explicated in relation to internal patterns of thought.

Meaning in history

The crucial question which needs to be raised to provide a foundation for a more explicitly historical, historical geography is 'What is a historical event?' or 'What criteria can be used to distinguish historical from nonhistorical actions?' One must distinguish a natural process governed by laws and theories from the evolution of human society (the historical process). It makes little sense to speak of 'historical' events in natural science because any natural process is described by laws that determine its outcome. These laws operate on and control every element of the natural process (or are assumed to do so). Human society is quite different. Human beings are bound by physical and biological laws, but their deliberate actions are not controlled by such laws. The human mind has taken an active role in shaping human society. Human beings, in brief, create their own rules of behaviour and through them change the nature of human existence. The historian has privileged access to the human past, because this past is concerned with the actions of reasoning beings like himself.[50] In viewing human society as a historical creation of the human mind one establishes a general criterion of historicity. The developments that are properly considered historical are those that have shaped the nature of human societies and their institutions.

The idealist idea of history contains a built-in criterion of historical significance that is loose enough to give individual scholars a large measure of freedom (for independent judgement) yet tight enough to give historical studies a specific identity that is separate from the natural and social sciences. This criterion is derived from the identification of history with thought. Any event, and the evidence on which it is reconstructed, that helps a historical scholar show how thought developed in a particular realm of human activity at a scale appropriate to his topic can be considered to be of potential historical significance. The focus on thought separates history from the sciences and provides it with its own principle for the organization of knowledge and a basis for individual judgement.

Although a historian can operate at different scales and focus on different topics, he is not like a scientist in that his concern is not with cause, but the logical development of mind. The explication of a historical episode becomes clearer and clearer by the historian providing more and more detail about the sequential development of the mind. A complete historical account would not be one in which an episode would be fully described in the sense of providing enough information to have made possible its prediction, but, rather, one in which there were no logical gaps describing the development of mind.

Oakeshott has put forward a clear statement on history conceived of as a full account of change.

It is a presupposition of history that every event is related and that every change is but a moment in a world which contains no absolute hiatus. And the only explanation of change relevant or possible in history is simply a complete account of change. History accounts for change by means of a full account of change. The relation between events is always other events, and it is established in history by a full relation of events. The conception of cause is thus replaced by the exhibition of a world of events intrinsically related to one another in which no lacuna is tolerated. To see all the degrees of change is to be in possession of a world of facts which calls for no further explanation. History, then, neither leaves change unexplained, nor attempts to explain it by an appeal to some external reason or universal cause: it is the narration of a course of events which, in so far as it is without serious interruption, explains itself. In history, *'pour savoir les choses, il faut savoir le détail'*. And the method of the historian is never to explain by means of generalization but always by means of greater and more complete detail.[51]

Any society is the end product of a historical process (not to be confused with a natural process). This process began when humans first emerged from the world of Nature and created laws and institutions to regulate their social and biological relations. The changing circumstances of various social groups

created new problems for which new solutions were devised. Each generation
was shaped by those preceding it, because the cultural heritage of the past
provided the base for change and new growth. All societies have been shaped
by the historic past. Although human society is a historical creation, it is not
controlled by its history in the sense that a natural phenomenon is controlled by
physical conditions. History remains the unpredictable outcome of the
constant interaction of individuals and groups seeking a social framework
within which their psychological, social and biological needs can be realized.

The basis of a historical analysis is a sense of history, by which I mean an
ability to identify problems in their historical contexts. The historian, or
historical geographer, is much like a detective who seeks to solve a crime.[52]
The detective must show how a wide variety of events are logically connected,
and support his construction with relevant evidence. In a historical problem
the questions might be different, but the procedures employed in solving them
are fundamentally the same. The historical equivalent of the detective's final
explanation in a criminal detective story is the explanatory historical
narrative.

The historical narrative will ideally be a complete account of a historical
development. Complete, not in the sense of including everything, but complete
in the sense that a detective story is complete when all the questions
surrounding a case have been satisfactorily answered. Essentially the same
criteria apply to the explanation of a historical episode such as the enclosure
movement in England. Historical studies are not quite as simple as detective
stories, and it is unlikely that full agreement will ever be reached as to the
significance of the contribution of various elements to the event in question.
Those facts that can be logically connected with changes in thought become
the facts of history. Can we understand accurately the significance of the past
on the basis of a few facts selected from an infinite number? The historian
would claim that such understanding is indeed possible, at least in theory; this
is the central problem for the philosopher of history.

Historical geography is conceived of as a fully historical form of enquiry.
The way people have used the earth has changed as other facets of human
existence have changed. A historical investigation of human activity on the
face of the earth would show how changes in such activity were related to the
problem situations of the people who initiated them. This type of investigation
implies that the historical geographer will be able to understand situations in
terms of ideas of those he investigates, but this understanding must not be
confused with geographical perception studies. He must examine all ideas (not
just geographical ones) which have shaped the character of human activity on
the earth.

A historical geographical investigation will seek to place geographical
change in an appropriate historical context. This task will involve elucidating
the implications and meaning of changes in human activity on the earth's

surface in relation to the historical evolution of society. For example, the activities of a group of hunters and gatherers would not be considered historical so long as these activities repeated themselves within an unchanging social and geographical context. A change in a group's geographical activity would, however, become historical as soon as it involved a new solution to an old or new problem with societal repercussions. Thus, for example, it would be a historical change if hunters and gatherers established trading relations with neighbouring cultivators, because it implies a re-ordering of the groups' geographical and economic relationships. The purpose of a good historical geographical study would, in fact, be to trace the nature of geographical change in its historical relationship to a group's institutional and social (including political and economic) development.

Human society is the creation of the human mind and changes to it are the result of human thought. Thought, therefore, provides the basis for deciding whether a geographical change is of historical importance. Geographical changes of historical significance are those that can in some way be related to changes in the way people interpret their position in society and environment. In short, a change must be reflected in the ideas and activity of individuals and groups to qualify as historical. Thought, in other words, provides the fundamental criterion for deciding which geographical events or actions are of potential historical importance.

In insisting that history is concerned with actions as expressions of thought, one does not deny historical status to natural and psychological phenomena.[53] Such phenomena, however, only become historically significant in relation to human ideas. For example, a volcanic eruption in itself would not be a historical event, but the actions of the inhabitants of its slopes might well be. Collingwood has clarified this idea.

Some 'events' of interest to the historian are not actions but the opposite, for which we have no English word: not *actiones* but *passiones*, instances of being acted upon. Thus the eruption of Vesuvius in A.D. 79 is to the historian a *passio* on the part of the people affected by it. It becomes an 'historical event' in so far as people were not merely affected by it, but reacted to this affection by actions of various kinds. The historian of the eruption is in reality the historian of these actions.[54]

The application of the procedures described above implies that there can be objective historical geographical knowledge, in the sense that a true account will be one in which the relationships between thought and action are interpreted correctly. For example, if one states that a group began trading with neighbours as a solution to food shortages, the explanation implies that this solution to the problem of food shortages was in fact worked out in the minds of the group under study. The historian, of course, could be wrong, and might interpret his evidence incorrectly. My point is that an explanation is aimed at providing a true account of historical change, and precisely because this aim is shared by others a critical debate can take place over the merits of specific interpretations.

The idea that truth is not attainable, at least in any final or permanent sense, is almost an article of faith among modern historians. However, this view must not be misinterpreted. Each generation of historians may indeed be required to rewrite history as new perspectives on the past are developed and as new evidence is discovered. The process of rewriting history, however, is cumulative rather than circular. For example, as a result of recent scholarship we know more about the Victorian period than we did a few decades ago. Ideas on this period will undoubtedly undergo modifications and changes as a result of future research, but no matter how drastic these modifications and changes, our state of knowledge will not return to the point at which it was before recent research was done. The situation has some similarities to knowledge in the natural sciences, where new theories and ideas are constantly replacing old ones. In this quest for knowledge certain advances are not reversible. For example, it is unlikely that the Copernican view of the solar system or the idea of evolution will be abandoned. The final truth may not be an attainable goal, but careful and imaginative scholarship is, it seems to me, capable of advancing our understanding in that direction.

Conclusion

A limiting concept of history is widely accepted by historical geographers, who have until recently been preoccupied with defining the geographical character of their work. Historical geographers have been content with an essentially temporal concept of history and few have adopted a concept of history that clearly establishes history as an independent field. Interest in history has been at a methodological rather than a philosophical level.

The tradition of conceiving of historical geography in geographical terms can be traced to the influence of the modern founders of historical geography, among whom Hartshorne, Sauer, Darby and Clark made crucial contributions. All of these scholars accepted a temporal idea of history in their definitions of historical geography. The emphasis of historical geography was on reconstruction and change at the physical level, the level of external appearances and associations. No differentiation was made between the past as such and the historic past. The emergence of a more humanistic approach to historical geography was not associated with the adoption of a new concept of history. Although humanist geographers have rejected the natural-scientific model of enquiry, they have generally retained the temporal concept of history.

A modern definition of historical geography must include a modern concept of history. Historical geography is conceived of as the history of human activity on the earth's surface. It is a historical discipline, as fully historical as any other field of historical enquiry. A key problem of such a historical

22   *Inadequate concepts in Historical Geography*

geography is distinguishing historical facts from other past facts. Although the historical geographer might begin his study with traditional methods of reconstruction, his final narrative could only become historical with reference to human ideas. He does not become a perception geographer, although perception studies could be important. This concept of history is basically concerned with (complete) interlocking systems of ideas (political, geographical, economic, social) that have shaped human activity on the land. The changes in any idea with geographical implications is of potential importance for an understanding of such activity. The task of the historical geographer is neither the description of physical changes in the landscape nor the investigation of ideas (including geographical ideas) as such, but the understanding of historical change in geographical activity.

References and notes

1 D. Harvey, *Explanation in geography* (London, Edward Arnold, 1969).
2 The rich literature in the philosophy of history includes (among many others) Herodotus, Livy, Tacitus, Descartes, Vico, Locke, Herder, Kant, Hegel, Marx, Dilthey, Rickert, Bury, Croce, Oakeshott, and Collingwood; not to mention any more recent philosophers. Surprisingly Hartshorne in *The nature of geography* makes no references to Kant's ideas about history outside of what is written in the introduction to his lectures on physical geography. More recently, Ernst and Merrens, in presenting ideas on the nature of history, make few references to original work in the philosophy of history where many of the issues they present have been discussed at length. See J. A. Ernst and H. R. Merrens, 'Praxis and theory in the writing of American historical geography', *Journal of Historical Geography*, **4** (1978), 277–90.
3 For example, an article by M. Billinge, 'In search of negativism: phenomenology and historical geography', *Journal of Historical Geography*, **3** (1977), 55–67.
4 One exception to this statement is R. C. Harris, 'Theory and synthesis in historical geography', *The Canadian Geographer*, **15** (1971), 157–72; another is the perceptive, but neglected, paper on idealism by Lowther. See G. R. Lowther, 'Idealist history and historical geography', *The Canadian Geographer*, No. 14 (1959), 31–6.
5 R. Hartshorne, *The nature of geography* (Lancaster, Pa., Association of American Geographers, 1939), p. 134.
6 *Ibid.*, p. 135.
7 R. Hartshorne, *Perspective on the nature of geography* (Chicago, Rand McNally, for the Association of American Geographers, 1959), p. 102.
8 Hartshorne, *Nature*, p. 188.
9 An example of a cross-sectional approach is H. C. Darby, *Domesday England* (Cambridge, Cambridge University Press, 1977).
10 Hartshorne, *Perspective*, p. 103.
11 C. O. Sauer, 'Foreword to historical geography', *Annals of the Association of American Geographers,* **31** (1941), 1–24.

12 *Ibid.,* 13.
13 *Ibid.,* 18.
14 *Ibid.,* 7.
15 *Ibid.,* 10.
16 H. C. Darby, 'On the relations of geography and history', *Transactions and Papers of the Institute of British Geographers,* **19** (1953), 1–11.
17 *Ibid.,* 6.
18 *Ibid.,* 7.
19 *Ibid.*
20 H. C. Darby, 'Historical geography', in H. P. R. Finberg (ed.), *Approaches to history* (Toronto, University of Toronto Press, 1962), pp. 127–56.
21 See D. W. Moodie and J. C. Lehr, 'Fact and theory in historical geography', *The Professional Geographer,* **18** (1976), 132–5 for an excellent analysis of the shortcomings of this concept of history.
22 A. H. Clark, 'Historical geography in North America', in A. R. H. Baker (ed.), *Progress in historical geography* (Newton Abbot, David and Charles, 1972), pp. 130–1.
23 A. H. Clark, 'Geographical change: a theme for economic history', *Journal of Economic History,* **20** (1960), 607–16. For critical assessments of Clark's concept of historical geography see D. W. Meinig, 'Prologue: Andrew Hill Clark, historical geographer' in J. R. Gibson (ed.), *European settlement and development in North America: essays on geographical change in honour and memory of Andrew Hill Clark* (Toronto, University of Toronto Press, 1978) pp. 3–26, and G. Wynn, 'W. F. Ganong, A. H. Clark and the historical geography of Maritime Canada', *Acadiensis,* **10,** (1981), 16–28.
24 A. H. Clark, 'Historical geography', in P. E. James and C. P. Jones (eds.), *American geography: inventory and prospect* (Syracuse; Syracuse University Press for the Association of American Geographers, 1954), p. 72.
25 *Ibid.*
26 *Ibid.,* p. 71.
27 *Ibid.,* p. 72.
28 R. G. Collingwood, *The idea of history* (New York, Oxford University Press, 1956), p. 216.
29 A. H. Clark, *Three centuries and the island* (Toronto, University of Toronto Press, 1959).
30 A. Koelsch, in *Economic Geography,* **46** (1970), 201–2; M. J. Bowden in *Economic Geography,* **46** (1970), 202–3; A. R. H. Baker, 'Rethinking historical geography', in Baker, *Progress,* pp. 11–28.
31 An example of this kind of diversity is R. Foster and O. Ranum (eds.), *Family and society: selections from the Annales, economies, sociétés, civilisations* (Baltimore, The Johns Hopkins University Press, 1976).
32 This concept has been promoted by the *Annales* school of French historiography.
33 Some of these developments are reviewed by A. R. H. Baker, 'Historical geography: a new beginning', *Progress in Human Geography,* **4** (1979), 560–70, and H. C. Prince, 'Historical geography in 1980', in E. H. Brown (ed.), *Geography yesterday and tomorrow* (Oxford, Oxford University Press, 1980), pp. 229–50.
34 J. K. Wright, *Human nature in geography* (Cambridge Mass., Harvard University Press, 1966) is a collection of Wright's essays.

35 *Ibid.*, p. 83.
36 See C. J. Glacken, *Traces on the Rhodian shore: nature and culture in Western thought from ancient times to the end of the eighteenth century* (Berkeley, University of California Press, 1967), and Y. F. Tuan, *The hydrological cycle and the wisdom of God: a theme in geoteleology* (Toronto, University of Toronto Press, 1967). See also D. Lowenthal and M.J. Bowden (eds.), *Geographies of the mind: essays in historical geography in honor of John Kirkland Wright* (New York, Oxford University Press, 1976)
37 T. Bunting and L. Guelke, 'Behavioral and perception geography a critical appraisal', *Annals of the Association of American Geographers,* **69** (1979), 448–62.
38 Billinge, 'In search of negativism', 66.
39 Harris, 'Theory and synthesis', 157–72; and R. C. Harris 'The historical mind and the practice of geography', in D. Ley and M. S. Samuels (eds.), *Humanistic geography* (Chicago, Maaroufa Press, 1978), pp. 123–37.
40 Harris, 'Mind', pp. 128–9.
41 Harris, 'Theory and synthesis', 159–60.
42 *Ibid.*, 166.
43 Billinge, 'In search of negativism', 56.
44 Ernst and Merrens, 'Praxis and theory', 288–9.
45 D. Gregory, *Ideology, science and human geography* (London, Hutchinson, 1978); ——, 'Rethinking historical geography', *Area* **8** (1976), 295–8; ——, 'The discourse of the past: phenomenology, structuralism and historical geography', *Journal of Historical Geography*, **4** (1978), 161–73.
46 Gregory, 'Discourse of the past', 161–73.
47 D. Gregory, 'Social change and spatial structures' in T. Carlstein, D. Parkes and N. Thrift (eds.), *Making sense of time* (New York, John Wiley, 1978), pp. 38–46.
48 D. W. Moodie and J. C. Lehr, 'Fact and theory', 132–5.
49 H. C. Prince 'Real, imagined and abstract worlds of the past', *Progress in Geography*, **3** (1971), 1–86.
50 T. G. Bergin and M. H. Fisch (eds.), *The new science of Giambattista Vico* (New York, Anchor Books, 1961), pp. 52–3.
51 M. Oakeshott, *Experience and its modes* (Cambridge, Cambridge University Press, 1933), p. 143.
52 Collingwood, *Idea of history*, pp. 266–8.
53 *Ibid.*, pp. 205–31.
54 R. G. Collingwood, *An Autobiography* (Oxford, Oxford University Press, 1938), p. 128.

2

Rational understanding

Historical geographers are concerned with human activity on the earth as the expression of ideas. The ideas that interest a historical geographer will be those that enable him to understand the nature of human geographical change. This concept of historical geography implies that the historical geographer is able to penetrate the minds of the people whom he is studying, and to uncover their historically meaningful thought. There is considerable scepticism about the possibility that a scholar can ever know the contents of another person's mind, let alone a person of another time and culture. It is necessary, therefore, to provide some indication of what is meant by rational understanding and how it can be accomplished.

A basic distinction can be drawn between what Collingwood termed the 'outside' and 'inside' of a human event.[1] The 'outside' refers to all human activity that a historian can describe in terms of bodies and their movements. In historical geography this might involve such things as human migrations and settlement patterns. The word 'inside' denotes those aspects of human activity that can only be described in terms of thought. Human migrations and settlement activity involve thought as much as they do physical movements: people act to accomplish purposeful goals, and their actions can be understood as geographical expressions of social priorities.

The historian, unlike the natural-scientist, is unable to understand the nature of human activity unless he is able to uncover the thought contained in it. He looks at a human action as a unity of its outside and inside, and must investigate both aspects. A historical account may indeed begin with an investigation of the outside of human actions, but the historical meaning of such activity will be a function of ideas.

The historical scholar is able to understand the activities of past societies because man is a reasoning animal. Rational thought differentiates human behaviour from that of other living things. Animals may have rationality, but only the human being has fundamentally altered his existence by his own imaginative efforts. The human being has undergone no major physiological changes over the past ten thousand years, so the changes wrought by man must be understood in terms of inventions and conventions that he himself has made.[2] The rational mind continues to be the crucial element behind the various forms of human activity on the land at the individual and societal levels. The objective of the historical geographer is to understand the nature of human activity on the earth by uncovering the thought expressed in it.

The nature of rational thought

The phenomena of the external world acquire their intellectual meaning for an individual in terms of his theoretical ideas. Data without theory are dead. A mind without theories is empty. I use the word 'theory' here to include any idea or system of ideas that man has invented, learned, imposed, or elicited from the raw data of sensation that make connections among the phenomena of the external world. Religions, myths, and ideologies are all examples of theories.

What is the essential nature of theoretical knowledge? A theory is a conjecture in which certain phenomena are related to each other in a definite manner. A theory will often contain certain categories that are not perceivable, but are inferred from observable data. An essential of all theoretical knowledge is the ability to recognize similarities and differences. A child's avoidance of fire after being burnt would be based on a recognition of a category of phenomena (fire) and on a postulation of a universal connection between fire and unpleasant personal injury. A single encounter with a phenomenon is often a sufficient basis for conjecturing a universal relationship between specified elements of it.[3]

Our theoretical knowledge of the world that enables us to negotiate its hazards successfully is acquired through a process of conjecture and refutation at an early age. This directly acquired common-sense theory includes obvious relationships between such elements as fire and burning, sugar and sweetening, and the like. However, this kind of stimulus–response thinking barely distinguishes humans from animals.

Each individual is heir to the ideas and traditions of the society into which he is born. The phenomena of the world acquire historical meaning and significance in terms of categories and relationships that one is taught. Actions might be classified as good or evil, land as public or private, and individual attributes might be related to nationality or ethnic origin. The naïve objects of experience become increasingly endowed with social, economic, and political significance. The world acquires new symbolic dimensions. The framework or system of thought that forms the basis of one's thinking is crucial to the way in which one will interpret the world. Facts are the slaves of the theories one holds.

The importance of human thought rests on its cumulative nature. Knowledge accumulated as human societies developed. New ideas developed on the basis of old ones. This process was fundamentally historical, because each new step rested on steps already taken. No society ever developed in a vacuum and no society has had the luxury of stepping, as it were, outside of history in formulating its conventions, laws and institutions. The unique historical experiences of groups and societies have created a multitude of distinctive human forms of life.

Let me cite examples of the use of theoretical systems in the interpretation of events. Many tribal societies have well-developed witchcraft theories of disease and personal injury. Evans-Pritchard has described some basic features of witchcraft theory:

As a natural philosophy it [witchcraft] reveals a theory of causation. Misfortune is due to witchcraft cooperating with natural forces. If a buffalo gores a man, or the supports of a granary are undermined by termites so that it falls on his head, or he is infected with cerebro-spinal meningitis, Azande say that the buffalo, the granary, and the disease, are causes which combine with witchcraft to kill a man. Witchcraft does not create the buffalo and the granary and the disease, for these exist in their own right, but it is responsible for the particular situation in which they are brought into lethal relations with a particular man. The granary would have fallen in any case, but since there was witchcraft present it fell at the particular moment when a certain man was resting beneath it. Of these causes the only one which permits intervention is witchcraft, for witchcraft emanates from a person. The buffalo and the granary do not allow of intervention and are, therefore, whilst recognized as causes, not considered the socially relevant ones.[4]

Empirical data can always be interpreted in ways which are consistent with the principles of witchcraft if one accepts these principles without question. A man who is ill will probably go to a professional 'witchdoctor', because 'witchdoctors' are the acknowledged experts in finding the individuals responsible for the illness of their clients, and for suggesting counter-measures against further suffering. If a patient succumbs while undergoing treatment his death can be attributed to exceptional ill will emanating from his enemies, but if he recovers the 'witchdoctor' can claim full credit. A 'witchdoctor' with a reputation for patients dying while undergoing treatment would lose his patients as surely as any European or North American doctor with a similar reputation.

Two important points about general theory can be elicited from this example. The way in which phenomena are interpreted depends on one's theoretical point of view; in witchcraft theory all personal injuries, including disease, fall within a single basic category. In the second place, there will normally be ways of explaining cases that apparently do not conform to one's general theories without having to question their truth. Just as the existence of quacks provides no grounds for abandoning our faith in medical science, so the failings of witchcraft can always be laid at the feet of an individual practitioner. Both witchcraft and modern medical science go beyond the naïvely observable phenomena. A disease – depending on the framework accepted – might be attributed to personal enemies or to germs. Both theories attempt to explain a concrete phenomenon in terms of entities that are not directly observable. The way in which the world is interpreted will be radically different, depending on the basic theoretical framework that is accepted.

Once a particular theoretical framework has been accepted, however, it is often extremely difficult for an individual to accept any other.[5] People believing in witchcraft theories would have their interpretation of the world revolutionized in changing to a germ theory of disease and a scientific world view. The categories of phenomena which derived their meaning from the witchcraft system of relationships would have to be abandoned as meaningless in relation to germ theory. In some cases the explanatory power of germ theory would be quite impressive when compared with witchcraft theory, but the gains in understanding would not always be positive. The witchcraft theory of misfortune, for example, had no difficulty in accounting for the fact that a buffalo gored one particular person. Western science might attribute the same incident to chance – a poor explanation from the point of view of the injured person. The idea that any theory is self-evidently true can only be entertained by those who have grown up with it. Germ theory would certainly not be self-evident to 'witchdoctors' any more than it was self-evident to the contemporaries of Semmelweis.

In the long run, theories that manage to pass genuine empirical tests can be expected to gain acceptance over other theories. In the physical and biological sciences one can anticipate the emergence of an increasingly uniform 'scientific' view in all areas of the world. Even in this most advanced section of scientific endeavour, however, rival theories can often hold sway for long periods. The introduction of ad-hoc hypotheses and reclassification of anomalous phenomena often enable rival theories, which give different interpretations of the same sets of data, to coexist in the scientific world. If no general agreement seems possible in an area where relatively dispassionate investigation is possible, how many unresolvable differences of theory can be expected in religion, politics, or social relationships?

The 'soft' nature of most social theory means that a number of theories are usually competing with each other to explain the same set of facts. A person who accepts the philosophical underpinnings of capitalism will be inclined to attach slight significance to such aspects of the system as unemployment or poverty. These phenomena might be seen as products of individual laziness and lack of initiative rather than as inevitable features of the system. The concept of poverty might well be replaced by a concept of degrees of wealth, with a view to denying that poverty as such constitutes a problem. A socialist, however, might interpret the same data as an indictment of the capitalist system. Unemployment and poverty might be interpreted as the deliberate and necessary creations of a social order based on the exploitation of the poor and disadvantaged by the rich and powerful. The significance of unemployment and the uneven distribution of wealth is related entirely to one's fundamental theoretical outlook. The evidence in favour of some theories is much stronger than the evidence in favour of others. The fact that certain key propositions are often accepted in self-interested, dogmatic fashion, tends to be more important than the uncertainties implicit in the actual evidence, and militates against rapid changes in established patterns of thought.

Thought and action I

The action of Christopher Columbus in setting out across the Atlantic Ocean is understood in terms of his expectation of reaching China by that route. This expectation was based on the acceptance of a theory that the earth was a sphere of a somewhat smaller circumference than it is. Columbus, in relation to the geographical and commercial notions he entertained, behaved in a rational manner in sailing westwards across the Atlantic. At one point in his investigations of the high death rate from puerperal fever in the Vienna General Hospital, Semmelweis directed a priest to dispense with his bell-ringing assistant. This request was made in the belief that the noise created by the bell, which was more noticeable in a ward with a higher incidence of fever, might be an indirect cause of the ward's high death rate. The notion that doctors might themselves have transmitted the fever while examining patients must have been as unthinkable to persons without knowledge of germ theory as we find the notion that sound and disease might be causally connected, yet in terms of his understanding Semmelweis clearly behaved in a rational way. One who cannot see that the actions of Columbus and Semmelweis were rationally connected to their beliefs is not capable of understanding their actions.[6]

The basic model of a rational explanation consists of two parts. First one must ascertain the intention of the agent in the action to be explained. An intention provides the occasion on which an individual will apply the theory that he regards as appropriate; knowledge of his intention is a prerequisite for understanding the theory-dependent actions employed towards its fulfillment. Intentions without theories are blind, theories without intentions are (behaviourally) empty. For example, a man stranded in a desert might desperately desire to find water, but his desire could not be translated into meaningful action without the appropriate theory to tell him what signs might be indicative of water. The actual form of an intention can only be understood in terms of the theory that was entertained at the time the intention was translated into action. The second and normally the major portion of a rational explanation is an understanding of the theoretical ideas that were employed by an agent in the interpretation of his situation. The goal of Semmelweis in investigating childbed fever can be described in a couple of sentences, but the various ways that he explored in trying to achieve it might fill a book.

The intention, desire, or goal of a rational agent need not be explained in order to understand the rational theory-dependent moves that were taken in trying to reach it. For example, one might understand the first voyage of Columbus in terms of his goal of reaching China without considering why he wanted to go there. A closed explanatory unit is formed by the statement of his goal and an elucidation of the theories that made a rational action of sailing across the Atlantic Ocean in a westerly direction. It answers completely the question: 'Why did Columbus voyage westward across the Atlantic Ocean?' If one desires to ask the question. 'Why did Columbus desire to go to China?' a new explanation is needed. Here the goal of the action might be specified as trading with profit. The selection of China rather than some other region would have to be understood in terms of the theoretical ideas that Columbus had about China's trade potential and the relative difficulties involved in getting there.[7] The goal of reaching China thus becomes a theoretical link in the attainment of a deeper purpose. The rational method of understanding is concerned with actions as expressions of ideas, not in discovering their psychological or biological genesis. This limitation of rational understanding is not a handicap for understanding human actions, which can be completely understood in relation to intentions that are not explained. There is no contradiction in the notion of a rational suicide.

The explanation of an action is complete when the agent's goal and theoretical understanding of his situation have been discovered. It is not necessary to investigate the grounds on which a particular theory might be entertained, because they are irrelevant to understanding an action that might be related to it. For example, one can have a rational understanding of why Columbus sailed west across the Atlantic Ocean without needing to know whether he believed that the earth was a sphere of a certain circumference because he deduced the fact from personal observation, or because he believed information in some old manuscripts, or because he was a latter-day Pythagorean. *One must discover what he believed*, not why he believed it. Similarly, one only has to know that Semmelweis believed that there might be a connection between noisy bells and childbed fever in order to understand his action. Although the grounds on which an idea is held do not themselves form part of the rational explanation, they frequently play an important role in supporting an explanation that has been given.

By re-thinking, one seeks to discover the way in which a geographical agent construed his situation in order to see the link between thought and action. Re-thinking the thoughts of other people does not involve some mystical operation of mind reading; it does not even require empathy in the usual sense. This method does require imagination and an ability to push one's own theories to the back of one's mind. To understand the actions of a peasant cultivator, for example, one would have to learn a completely new set of theories. Once one had grasped the principles on which the cultivator interpreted his world, his actions in specific situations would become intelligible. Rational understanding involves seeing the sense of an action, and can therefore be used to understand situations that have only occurred once. A single unique situation can be understood as well as one that had been repeated a thousand times.[8]

The rational understanding of an event leaves everything precisely as it was. The human geographer attempts to reconstruct the thought expressed in the actions that were taken. He does *not* need theories of his own, because he is concerned with the theories expressed in the actions of the individual being investigated. The form of human actions largely reflects how people understand their situation, and their actions must be understood in relation to that understanding. Human situations, in which developments are governed by the internal principles of the agents involved in them, are not explained in a satisfactory manner by attempting to establish relationships among categories that have been imposed on them by the analyst himself. This positivist or natural-scientific approach is admirably suited to the study of nonrational phenomena, but it is inappropriate to the investigation of activities which are themselves the products of theoretical understanding.

A historical geographer will frequently attempt to increase his understanding of the strategy that was actually adopted by exploring the alternatives. Such an investigation would show why the courses of action that were adopted were judged most appropriate. A similar procedure is often employed in understanding the moves in a game such as chess. It can usually be established that the players are familiar with the rules of the game, and desire to win it. The various moves will be related to each player's understanding of his situation at various times, and the strategy he adopts to meet the needs of these situations. A good move will be one that fully meets the needs of a particular situation. A commentator might elucidate a move that seemed poorly thought out in two different ways. He might rebut the presumption that the move was inappropriate by showing that all other possible moves were even less advantageous, or might show that the situation that developed out of it was not foreseen. The failure of a player to see the possibilities of a situation might be attributed to his lack of intelligence, his inexperience, or to his emotional state. These kinds of statements constitute the grounds on which an interpretation of a certain move might be supported.

In the case of chess, a commentator must be knowledgeable of the game if he is going to follow what each player is doing and be able to elucidate the strategies adopted. But a good commentator needs to go beyond understanding to criticism. He is required to criticize players for missing opportunities or failing to develop adequate strategies. Criticism, however, can only be effective where the commentator himself is capable of evaluating alternative strategies. He will then be able to demonstrate exactly why a particular strategy failed or show where an opportunity for making a winning move was missed.

The historian has a similar role to that of a commentator. He must evaluate historical actions in relation to the ideas they express and criticize them. Unlike a game, in history the rules of action are not fixed and a historian has the more difficult task of evaluating human actions in situations in which the 'rules' are changing. Like a commentator, a historian must be knowledgeable about the situation he investigates in order to provide an adequate evaluation of them. He can criticize an action or policy if he is able to show that it failed to achieve its objectives, but he should not criticize on the basis of hindsight. In elucidating a human action it is necessary to distinguish between developments occurring after a certain decision that were, in principle, anticipatable when the decision was taken, and those that were not. If an action was clearly detrimental to the known objectives of an agent, one might elucidate it by showing that the theory available to the agent when the decision was taken was not powerful enough to provide an adequate analysis of the situation, or that the data on which he based the decision was incomplete. It would, for example, be ridiculous to hold the Vienna doctors of Semmelweis's day responsible for the deaths of the mothers who succumbed to childbed fever, because they were performing their duties in a way that was at that time regarded as correct. An individual must always act in the light of accepted beliefs, which at any time may be falsified by empirical findings.

Thought and action II

If it is conceded that, in principle, a human action is explained when the thought it contains has been understood, this mode of understanding must be equally applicable to the actions of great and ordinary people. The question 'Why did Brutus stab Ceasar?' and the question 'Why did a farmer plant soybeans last year?' must be answered in precisely the same way. The major difficulty in applying the rational model of understanding to the behaviour of ordinary people is the vast number of actions that involve this type of person. A political movement might be the expression of millions of individual decisions, which it would be clearly impossible to re-think one by one. Does this mean that rational understanding is not applicable to geography, which is often concerned with the actions of ordinary people?[9] I do not think so. The problem posed here is at the level of methodology rather than at the level of philosophy. The necessity of understanding the thought in actions is still insisted upon, but methods are devised to handle cases in which this cannot be done on an individual basis.

A single theory can have an effect on the actions of countless individuals if they all understand certain situations in terms of it. For example, the fact that surgeons are careful to disinfect their hands before operating on their patients is understood in terms of their belief in the existence of harmful germs. A surgeon may not consciously think about what he is doing every time he is about to perform an operation, but his actions are not mere habit. He understands that his failure to do certain things would reduce the chances of a successful operation. His actions are based on a theoretical understanding of his actual situation. If we wish to explain why thousands of surgeons disinfect their hands before performing operations we only have to show that all have understood the implications of the germ theory of disease. Assume that the surgeons' actions are not related to germ theory. Would it make any sense for a surgeon who did not believe in germs to take precautions against them? Obviously not. Indeed, the high death rate that resulted from unsterile conditions before the germ theory of disease was elaborated is clear evidence in favour of this analysis. In focusing on a specific action one is only obliged to uncover the thought that is relevant to it; all other distinctive aspects of an individual's thought can be ignored if they are unrelated to the action.

A rational human action is the product of individual understanding, even when repeated many times. The human being is not seen as the helpless victim of external forces beyond his control, but as a rational agent actively imposing theoretical order on the world in pursuit of goals that are themselves a product of conscious thought.

The idealist approach to the explanation of human actions does not neglect the material aspects of human existence, but it does insist that they be treated in relation to the thought of the individuals involved. Individuals are seen as holding their own places in society. Their actions are related to their rational understanding of their own situations and to an appreciation of the possibilities inherent in them. If the material conditions of a social group are changed, the adjustments in their social order must be understood in terms of the rational responses of the people affected by the changes. An example of a rational response to new conditions is provided by the Mennonite groups that settled Manitoba in the late nineteenth and early twentieth centuries. These groups re-created the nucleated villages of their Russian homeland, but the areas on which the villages and communal farm lands were set out were legally assigned to individuals. The members of each group voluntarily pooled their land so that they could continue to farm along traditional lines. It did not take long, however, for certain individuals to exploit the possibility, implicit in their new situation, of breaking away from the group and setting themselves up on their own land. This process eventually led to the breakdown of the Mennonites' traditional communal villages. If a change in an individual's situation does occur, however, it is historically significant only to the extent that he himself recognizes the possibilities resulting from the change.

There is no objective historical reality that is independent of the historical agents themselves. The idea that humans have made themselves is contradicted by the idea that they are made by an 'objective' reality whether they know it or not. The only knowledge that can be considered historical knowledge is knowledge that is self-consciously known. History is an account of the world as it was known and shaped by human ideas. A phenomenon such as class only exists where people think of themselves in class terms. A historian is not required to define concepts like class, nationality, religion, ethnicity or race. The historical significance of such categories is defined by people making history, not by professors in their studies. Where a historian claims that class or ethnicity has a historical importance, he must support this claim with logical argument and empirical evidence.

The social relations of societies are a reflection of self-conscious understanding. These relations must be understood as the historical creations of people themselves. Although people make themselves, they do so in concrete situations. All people are to some extent 'victims' of circumstance. To say this is not to deny people creative freedom, but to place limits on what is possible in specific historical situations. The limits of freedom, however, do not exist as 'objective' facts but as ideas in the mind. There is no such thing as an objective situation that can be understood without reference to the ideas of the people comprising it.

In insisting that historical situations be understood in terms of self-consciously held ideas, one does not deny the existence of an external reality. The historian is an observer of history as an external spectacle. The reconstructions of the external manifestations of historical episodes and events is a proper task of the historical scholar. A historical geographer, for example, needs to know such things as where people moved, the patterns of settlement, or the rate of urban growth. The spectacle itself, however, is not history. It becomes history when someone is able to interpret the spectacle as a reflection of human ideas.

History is a study of how actions are connected from the inside, in terms of the logical development of thought. It is no objection to the idealist position to point out that the same events look different when analysed from another point of view. There is no problem for the idealist historian trying to reconcile two (or more) points of view, because the historian has only one point of view to contend with in making sense of the past, namely that of the historical agents themselves.

The writing of history is a second order, reflective activity. The events of the past are not changed by historical investigations. Historical knowledge is a purely intellectual knowledge of no direct practical value. Historical understanding is knowledge for its own sake. The knowledge of the past can aspire to objectivity, precisely because the historian is concerned to understand the world not to change it. Historical knowledge as knowledge for its own sake is differentiated from the study of the past with practical aims in mind. The use of the past to inculcate patriotism or to establish claims on territory distorts the intellectual goals of history and makes any kind of objectivity all but impossible. This kind of history might itself become the object of historical analysis, as a reflection of how a society construed itself.

Verification

Although the historian is required, because of the nature of thought, to reconstruct the thought of an individual from external evidence, his interpretations need not be subjective personal opinion. There are appropriate, rigorous, and intellectually responsible procedures for testing the worth of any interpretation of an individual's activities. Even if an interpretation passes all the tests, of course, one can never guarantee that it corresponds to the real thoughts of the individual, but the situation in the physical sciences is no different:

We can never establish with certainty that a given theory is true, and that the entities it posits are real. But to say that is not to disclose a peculiar flaw in our claims about theoretical entities, but to note a pervasive characteristic of all empirical knowledge.[10]

There are similarities between scientific theories and rational interpretations with regard to criteria of acceptability. Scientific theories and historical interpretations of actions in terms of thought both attempt to understand situations by postulating the existence of nonperceivable entities. A physicist will use concepts like electron and proton in order to explain the electrical and magnetic properties of materials. The only evidence to suggest that such entities exist is obtained indirectly; an electron is a theoretical construct from observed data. A historical interpretation attempts to construct a pattern of thought that fits the observable manifestations of an individual's behaviour. Both the physicist and the idealist historical geographer are involved in the creation of constructions that are inferred from empirical evidence.

Theories and interpretations can be assessed in somewhat similar ways. A good theory will explain a host of phenomena of a certain kind. Ad-hoc hypotheses to protect theories from refutation are always suspect. A good interpretation will identify underlying thought patterns which enable one to explain a large number of actions in which an individual is involved. Ad-hoc interpretations usually warrant close scrutiny. Unlike a physical theory which can, in principle, be refuted by one well-confirmed negative instance, an interpretation will seldom be refuted on the basis of a single action that is inconsistent with one's interpretation of an agent's thought pattern. An interpretation in terms of an underlying theory or pervasive influence which is in continual need of additional ad-hoc hypotheses will be highly suspect, however, unless it is extraordinarily well supported by empirical evidence.

The similarities between the scientist and historian must not be pressed too far. The historian, unlike the scientist has no interest in prediction and is in no position to prove his conclusions in the same way that a scientist is able to demonstrate an idea with an experiment. The historian is able to justify his account of the past by establishing a logical narrative connecting events. This narrative must be supported wherever possible by hard evidence. The historian, in other words, seeks to produce a coherent account of change appealing both to logic and to facts. The historical narrative can be challenged on the grounds of faulty logic, inadequate or incomplete evidence or both. There can be no history in the absence of evidence. The 'real' past is nothing other than the past that the evidence obliges us to accept. Where a historian is dealing with a fragmentary record, he must use whatever techniques he has at his disposal to extract all the information possible from it.

Conclusion

The idea that human geographers ought to attempt to emulate natural and social scientists in search of theory overlooks the fact that man himself is a theoretical animal whose actions are based on the theoretical understanding of his situation. As man's theoretical ideas change, so will his behaviour. The idealist philosophy gives historical geographers an approach to understanding that allows them to take full account of the special nature of human theoretical behaviour. Re-thinking the thoughts of people whose action he wishes to explain enables the scholar to understand human actions in a critical analytical way without theory. Verification procedures open to critical examination are available to test the validity of such interpretations. The historical geographer aims at providing coherent narrative accounts of the situations he investigates, supporting them with appropriate empirical evidence.

References and notes

1 R. G. Collingwood, *The idea of history* (New York, Oxford University Press, 1956), p. 213.
2 There would appear to be a limit to the phenomena that can be explained by the scientific method. Are scientists able to give scientific explanations of their own work? Any ultimate theory of scientific knowledge would have to account for its own existence if the possibility of scientific explanations of all phenomena is not to be regarded as limited.
3 This idea comes from K. Popper, *Conjectures and refutations*, 2nd edn (New York, Basic Books, 1965), pp. 33–59.
4 E. E. Evans-Pritchard, 'Witchcraft', *Africa*, **8** (1935), 418–19.
5 Lord Kelvin, for example, when faced with irrefutable evidence that fossils predated the creation of the earth (according to the Bible) suggested that God created the fossil evidence at the same time that he created the earth with a view to testing our faith in the Bible.
6 Both actions can be understood as unique cases.
7 The desire to reach China must have been present before the theory by which it was rendered a feasible undertaking was known.
8 Walsh is incorrect in suggesting that one would need to know how a people commonly reacted to a given situation before one could understand their behaviour.

W. H. Walsh, *Philosophy of history*, 2nd edn (New York, Harper and Row, 1967), p. 57.

9 The extent to which human geographers are involved with ordinary people should not, however, be exaggerated. Decisions of historical significance are often taken by individuals and relatively small groups of people.

10 C. Hempel, *Philosophy of natural science* (Englewood Cliffs, N.J., Prentice-Hall, 1966), p. 80.

3

Objections to the concept of rational understanding

The notion that rational understanding might be the foundation of a viable approach to history has been widely criticized. Among common misconceptions are the notions that rational understanding is synonymous with economic rationality, that a scholar is required to identify himself emotionally with those whose actions he seeks to explain, and that re-enactment of thought involves the impossible task of recovering the full content of another's mind. Such misinterpretations of what re-enacting thought entails are relatively easy to rebut. There are also more serious objections to this view. Among such objections is the argument that human behaviour cannot be adequately understood by merely investigating thought, that the exclusion of subconscious motivations is a serious shortcoming of the approach, that there are no valid criteria on which historical interpretations can be verified, and that the approach, in lacking a clear commitment to theory, is necessarily subjective.

Misconceptions

The word 'rational' is often used as a synonym for 'economically rational', and in Western culture the rationality of an action is frequently assessed on economic criteria. This conception of rational is not altogether unsatisfactory in modern Western societies in which decisions are frequently based on economic considerations, but it is a completely unacceptable definition of the concept 'rational'. A rational action is the considered action of a thinking person; it is not restricted to an examination of economic elements, even less to an idealized simplification of them. There is no reason to consider the actions of, say, medieval people irrational, because their actions do not conform to our modern concepts of economic rationality. The thought of peoples of other cultures and ages must be assessed in terms of their beliefs and objectives if its rational character is to be appreciated.

The actions of a witchdoctor are, under this criterion, basically rational and his thought can be understood by those prepared to investigate the assumptions behind it. Actions which might be considered irrational by one criterion might be rational by another. The tribesmen who work for a limited time to acquire certain specific goods behave irrationally in terms of conventional economic theory. When wages are raised they respond by working fewer hours. They do not respond to 'economic incentives'. Yet is their behaviour irrational? Is it irrational for an individual to have certain fixed material goals, when his status within his society is not dependent on such goods, and traditional ideas discourage their accumulation? This behaviour fails to fit economic theory, but to label it irrational is to mistake an economic model of limited historical and geographical applicability for a universal truth.

The re-thinking of thought has nothing to do with sympathy or empathy, although an appreciation of an individual's emotional state can sometimes provide clues to his thought. The concept 're-thinking' is often explained as 'putting yourself in somebody else's shoes'. This description is somewhat confusing, because it fails to distinguish between thought and emotions. The scholar is interested in re-creating the thought in an action. The question, for example, of farm abandonment in nineteenth-century New England would be approached by the historical geographer seeking to show that the actions of those who left were based upon rational considerations of their positions. The scholar is not interested in re-experiencing or even trying to re-experience the emotional state of historical agents. The historical novelist might seek to describe how a farmer felt as he closed the farm gate for the last time, but the historical geographer limits himself to the strategic considerations that prompted this action and its economic and social meaning.

Re-thinking is, perhaps, best described as imaginative understanding. It is based upon a critical assessment of the evidence relating to an action. Collingwood stated:

It [re-enactment of thought] is not a passive surrender to the spell of another's mind; it is a labour of active and therefore critical thinking. The historian not only re-enacts past thought, he re-enacts it in the context of his own knowledge and therefore, in re-enacting it, criticizes it, forms his own judgement of its value, corrects whatever errors he can discern in it. This criticism of the thought whose history he traces is not something secondary to tracing the history of it. It is an indispensable condition of the historical knowledge itself. Nothing could be a completer error concerning the history of thought than to suppose that the historian as such merely ascertains 'what so-and-so thought', leaving it to some one else to decide 'whether it was true'. All thinking is critical thinking; the thought which re-enacts past thoughts, therefore, criticizes them in re-enacting them.[1]

Re-thinking is differentiated from empathy or sympathy because it is concerned with the rational component of thought, and because any inferences drawn about that thought need to be supported with appropriate documentation and arguments.

The idea of re-thinking does not imply that a scholar is required to re-enact all the thought of an individual historical actor. In most situations the elucidation of thought will involve identifying the purpose of an action within its historical context. An example of such elucidation is provided by Collingwood himself in his work on Roman Britain.[2] The problem Collingwood faced was how to account for a low mound that archaeologists had found running parallel to Hadrian's wall on its southern side. The idea that the mound called 'the Vallum', might have served a defensive function was rejected because it lacked the necessary dimensions and associated fortifications of a defensive barrier. Instead, Collingwood argued that the mound was a customs barrier for traffic passing between the north and south. Although the wall itself might have served both defensive and administrative functions, Collingwood maintained the mound was built to prevent jurisdictional problems between military and civilian authorities. In this case, the evidence on which these inferences have been made is quite thin, but the proposed explanation does accord with available evidence; it fits the facts.

The example just cited demonstrates how the 're-thinking' approach might be applied in an actual historical study. The essence of Collingwood's approach has been well summarized by Goldstein.

If Collingwood's solution to the Vallum problem is correct, there is a clear sense in which he has re-thought the thoughts of Hadrian in all of their historically-relevant character. The essential considerations which presumably passed through Hadrian's mind as he came to the decision to have the Vallum built have passed through Collingwood's as well. There is no suggestion of his having entered fully into the existential experience of the historical actor in the sense of reproducing the feelings, emotions, and other appurtenances of existing-and-experiencing-here-and-now in the way that an historical novelist might seek to do. Here, it seems, is the central feature of what Collingwood thinks history is: it is re-thinking thought on the basis of evidence without ever becoming psychology. As re-thinking thought, its object is what can be detached from the original context of action and be reproduced in the later context of historical inquiry, hence its object is universal and not existential.[3]

Although a historical approach is here put forward as an alternative to the theoretical approach of the formal sciences, it should not be considered to be theoryless in the ordinary sense of the word. A scholar will present an interpretation of an action in terms of the thought contained in it. Such an interpretation might be designated a 'theory' in the broadest sense. For example, Collingwood's idea that the Vallum was constructed to avoid jurisdictional problems, although clearly referring back to the mind of Hadrian, might be described as Collingwood's theory or interpretation of the Vallum. Although in ordinary language a theory can be used to refer to an interpretation or conjecture, such usage should not mislead anyone to think that this kind of explanation or elucidation has anything to do with the theoretical explanations of the formal sciences. In a formal sense, the idealist presents theoryless explanations, that is explanations that are not dependent (except indirectly) on the existence of theories or laws for their power and validity. The power of a historical interpretation of human action rests on the ability of a scholar to grasp a rational connection between thought and action; its validity or credibility is related to the strength of the evidence on which it is based.

The idealist will use theories indirectly to establish what happened in specific situations. Here the use of theories and laws relates primarily to reconstructing the external or outside aspects of human actions. The historical scholar will, for example, assume that the laws of physics as we know them were valid when Hadrian built the Vallum. For making assumptions of this kind one simply reaffirms the nonhistorical character of physical constants in human affairs. The issue of historical interest is not the constants (laws) of matter and life, but what humans have made of such constants. As Collingwood noted:

The fact that certain people live, for example, on an island has in itself no effect on their history; what has an effect is the way they conceive that insular position; whether for example they regard the sea as a barrier or as a highway to traffic. Had it been otherwise, their insular position, being a constant fact, would have produced a constant effect on their historical life; whereas it will produce one effect if they have not mastered the art of navigation, a different effect if they have mastered it better than their neighbours, a third if they have mastered it worse than their neighbours, and a fourth if every one uses aeroplanes. In itself, it is merely a raw material for historical activity, and the character of historical life depends on how this raw material is used.[4]

Re-thinking and causal explanation

Although many scholars readily admit the importance of thought for an understanding of historical situations, they consider that thought comprises but one element of historical reality. The idealist conception of historical knowing is considered far too narrow if an adequate understanding of a historical event is to be achieved. An exclusive concentration on thought prevents the historian from providing an adequate explanation of an event, because he is unable to identify all the relevant factors behind its occurrence. This criticism assumes that the task of the historian is identical to that of the natural scientist, and that both want to show that an event was the inevitable outcome of a specific set of initial conditions and laws. The historian's task is not comparable to that of the natural or social scientist and should not be assessed against criteria taken from such sciences.

Collingwood in *The idea of history* was proposing a radically different concept of explanation in history. In fact, it is probably best not to use the term 'explanation' for the kind of understanding involved in historical enquiry. The historian is concerned to elucidate the meaning of human activity, rather than explain it. There is no attempt to give an account of an event that is complete as this term is understood in the natural sciences. The historian is not concerned with providing a full explanation of an event, in the sense of providing enough information to have made possible its prediction.

These fundamental differences between history and science are dealt with by Collingwood, who wrote:

the historian need not and cannot (without ceasing to be a historian) emulate the scientist in searching for the causes or laws of events. For science, the event is discovered by perceiving it, and the further search for its cause is conducted by assigning it to its class and determining the relation between that class and others.[5]

The historian seeks to understand an event in terms of the thought expressed in it. This kind of understanding is the historical equivalent of the formal scientist's explanation, although of a quite different form. Collingwood made it clear that discerning the thought in action is not a step towards an explanation: it is the explanation.

To discover the thought is already to understand it. After the historian has ascertained the facts, there is no further process of inquiring into causes. When he knows what happened, he already knows why it happened.[6]

The above proposition rests, as is made clear in the next paragraph of *The idea of history*, on considering thought as a kind of cause, but the word 'cause' is used in a sense not encountered in the sciences. Collingwood wrote:

The cause of an event, for him [the historian], means the thought in the mind of the person by whose agency the event came about: and this is not something other than the event, it is the inside of the event itself.[7]

If an event involves a number of persons, the task of the historian is to elucidate the actions of the participants in terms of their situations and beliefs.

The elimination from history of cause, as this term is understood in the natural and social sciences, needs further clarification. It means that historians do not use theories from natural or social science in their interpretations. A historical geographer, for example, need not concern himself with the chemistry of soils in providing an account of declining crop yields in medieval England. He is concerned with the actions of those who might have been affected by this phenomenon. These actions need to be understood in terms of the ideas and circumstances of the inhabitants of medieval England. Whether medieval agriculturalists actually farmed in a manner that denuded the soil is not historically important; how they themselves construed their own actions is the only question that matters.

The philosopher of history, L. O. Mink, has clarified why historians can afford to ignore scientific explanations of physical phenomena.

But although an historian may explain this [why a particular method of farming exhausts the soil] in his lust to instruct at all costs, in what context of historical questions must he do so? Must he explain the aerodynamics of sailing as an essential part of his account of the defeat of the Spanish Armada by the swifter and more maneuverable English men-of-war? If so, we should have to say that this event is still not historically understood, to the extent that the physics of sailing against the wind has only recently been investigated and is still imperfectly known – and historians could most appropriately pursue their research into the English victory by conducting wind-tunnel experiments. The fact is that for Collingwood the question, 'Why did this method of farming exhaust the soil?' is not an historical question, though couched in the past tense. 'Why did people adopt and retain this method?' is an historical question.[8]

Notwithstanding the nonhistorical character of scientific causal explanations of physical and other phenomena, a historian might include a scientific account of such phenomena not necessarily 'to instruct at all costs', but rather to add a sense of drama to his narrative. If the reader is made aware of the 'real' causes of a phenomenon, he will often be able to see more clearly why it was not, and perhaps could not, be understood by people lacking certain modern scientific concepts. For example, the failure of the surgeons of Semmelweis's day to discover a connection between childbed fever and unsterile conditions is more easily understood when their theories of disease are contrasted with modern ideas. The use of modern knowledge of physical, biological or social processes in a historical narrative, however, would be for illustrative, dramatic or heuristic purposes and would play no logical role in the historical narrative proper.

In addition to their illustrative role, natural and social sciences can also be employed in the subsidiary role of establishing and checking historical facts. This role will be of greatest value in adding evidence against which contemporary actions may be assessed. There is no limit to the sorts of things that might become historical evidence. For example, in assessing the early accounts of the American West, one might wish to know whether the description of early travellers were mainly a reflection of their own experience in subhumid areas or an accurate account of the physical reality. A crucial question in such an investigation would be the likely state of the area when it was crossed. This reconstruction would be established using anything the geographer could lay his hands on, from tree ring analysis to buffalo migration patterns.

In insisting that historical understanding is not based upon natural science or social theory, I do not wish to place a limit on the topics of investigation. The study of the history of soils, for example, is a legitimate and proper study, but this kind of study belongs to the realm of natural science. Although humans' activity might well have created many kinds of soil, their contribution can be understood in physical, biological, and chemical terms. There is no need for the soil scientist to consider why land was cleared or fertilized to explain what the impact of these actions might have been. The natural scientist has little need of the history of historians, and the historical geographer can only use the results of the sciences in a limited way. In his concern with thought, the historian or historical geographer does not improve the logic of his analysis with scientific digressions that are unrelated to contemporary thought, but might make it more easily understandable to modern readers.

The idea of rational understanding in history has been widely criticized for ignoring the subconscious elements of human behaviour.[9] Basically the criticism suggests that human beings are not as rational as some have imagined, and that many of our actions are not the result of rational calculation at all.[10] Although such actions might be rationalized, their actual inspiration or driving force is to be found in the depths of the psyche or irrational mind. This criticism is again based upon an assumption that a historical explanation should, along the lines of a natural-scientific one, set out all the factors behind the occurrence of an event, including, of course, any nonrational psychological motivations. If we construe the task of the historian as elucidation rather than explanation, the inability of the idealist historian to uncover the subconscious mind is not a serious problem, or indeed a problem at all.

The rationality or intelligence of human beings has not freed them from their bodily existence with its psychological and physical drives and needs. The human intelligence has been harnessed to the fulfillment of these drives and needs, which are not classifiable as either rational or irrational. Thus, most human goals can ultimately be linked to psychological needs or desires, but this is not the concern of the historian. His concern is with the meaning actions acquire in specific historical contexts. The psychological basis of a leader's quest for power is not of historical importance, but the way in which he translated his desire for power into actual policy might well be. In other words, a desire or disposition is blind until it finds expression as a rational action in a specific context. The historical understanding of such an action is not dependent on discovering its 'real' cause any more than the historical understanding of medieval agriculture is dependent on modern soil science.

The emotions such as ambitiousness or anger are impossible to re-experience, or re-think, but they are not ignored in Collingwood's theory of history. An emotion is incorporated in the process of rational thought. An emotion survives in the actions and thought expressing it. In Collingwood's theory of mind there are levels of experience. The conscious level of thought does not supersede the level below it, but transforms it according to a new principle of organization.[11] For example, an individual may be angry or frustrated. As an emotion, anger is a fleeting state of consciousness that cannot be re-enacted. However, this anger might be 'rationally' expressed by someone kicking a dog or throwing a book at the wall. Kicking a dog is not irrational; it expresses anger in a way that is designed to give some positive sense of satisfaction to the angry person. In the same way ambitiousness is reflected in ambitious policy. We identify the psychological state in terms of rational actions which express it.

The historian is not concerned with unconscious motivations as causes of behaviour unless contemporary society interprets actions in terms of them. Freud's theories of the unconscious are not considered important because they undermine Collingwood's idea of history (which they do not), but because the theories themselves, in providing twentieth-century society with a new image of itself, are of potential historical significance in their own right. The 'unconscious' enters history as a concept whose impact on society the historian can evaluate using the method of re-thinking.

The historical scholar deals with events that have happened and that can never be changed. He knows the results of elections, migrations, settlements and revolutions. This knowledge places the historian in a very different position from other scholars. For the historian, theory is superfluous for interpretation (but is of course, vital in establishing what happened). An economist needs theory to predict the impact of, say, higher interest rates; a planner to predict traffic flows. Each of us needs theory to negotiate the world. Historical knowledge is not of this kind; it is not needed in contending with the future. The historian's task is to understand what happened, not to show that what happened had to happen. Historical understanding is essentially a commentary on the meaning of the past conceived of as a reflection of human ideas and priorities. The historian is concerned with the meaning of change at the level of self-conscious rational thought.

The nonrational element of mind takes on more significance in extreme cases, but even in such cases it is the meaning given to unconventional or erratic behaviour that is of crucial significance for a historian, not its physiological or psychological foundations. This point can be illustrated by an examination of the treatment of those we would today consider as mentally disturbed people. In earlier times such people were frequently considered 'possessed'. Their actions were construed religiously as manifestations of 'the devil', and they were treated as being responsible for their own condition, a condition rendered even more miserable by the attitudes of their contemporaries. Today, the mentally insane (or those recognized as such) have a somewhat less difficult ordeal under the conventional world scientific view which absolves them of personal responsibility for their behaviour. The condition of insanity (defined broadly or classified according to different symptoms or manifestations it might have) has not changed, but the meaning given to it certainly has. This meaning is basically a function of ideas, of accepted views and theories, and it is these ideas which ultimately shape the character of a society.

'All history is the history of thought'

When Collingwood stated 'all history is the history of thought' he provided a crucial criterion of historical significance. It is not possible to take a middle position on this central principle of historical knowledge. The idea that re-enacting thought might be valuable in some situations and less valuable in others misses the essence of this concept of history. The central issue of historical understanding is not how to explain this or that action or event, but deciding which actions or events should be included in a particular history. The attention given to such events as the colonial settlement of New England is easily accounted for within an idealist philosophy of history, less easily within a natural-scientific one. The English settlement of New England is important because it led to the triumph of a new ideology and world view and the demise of an old one. A materialist justification of this series of events might emphasize the number of lives disrupted, or behavioural patterns changed. On such a criterion, some of the devastating Chinese floods, or Indian famines might well qualify as historic events, as important, if not more so, than the early colonial settlements in New England. On a criterion of historical meaning these catastrophic events might not even qualify as historical at all.

The essence of a good historical geography is not related to how good the explanations of individual actions are, but rather to the actions the historical geographer decides to include in his narrative. A detailed examination of the causes of historically unimportant events would not constitute an adequate historical geography, no matter how good the explanations of each one might be. Philosophers and historians have in recent years become preoccupied with the problems of causal explanation to the neglect of the even more basic question of which actions qualify as historical events. Collingwood's statement 'all history is the history of thought' provides a basic criterion of historicity of fundamental importance for differentiating phenomena of historical importance from other phenomena. On this criterion it is the human mind that determines which actions will qualify as being of historical importance.

The importance Collingwood attributes to the re-enactment of thought as the crucial foundation of historical understanding leads him to deny a historical existence to primitive people. This denial should not be interpreted as the prejudice of a modern European, but as an essential implication of the idea that history is concerned with the world man has made for himself. In discussing early people Collingwood wrote:

The historicity of very primitive societies is not easily distinguishable from the merely instinctive life of societies in which rationality is at vanishing-point. When the occasions on which thinking is done, and the kinds of things about which it is done, become more frequent and more essential to the life of society, the historic inheritance of thought, preserved by historical knowledge of what has been thought before, becomes more considerable, and with its development the development of a specifically rational life begins.[12]

Collingwood was stating that the historian can do little in the way of re-thinking thoughts in the absence of a framework of thought within which society can develop. In such cases, each generation repeats what other generations have done before them, and such a repetition does not constitute history. Whether, in fact, many such societies ever existed is a question that does not affect the basic thrust of this argument.

The historian is interested in the way in which a specific historically-conditioned society interprets an event or phenomenon, not in a scientifically accurate account of it. An analysis of the causes of the Black Death, however interesting, is not historically important for an understanding of its impacts on medieval Europe. The historically interesting question is 'What does this episode tell us about the nature of medieval society?' How did the assumptions, values and ideas accepted by this society shape its response to this phenomenon? The historian, to get at these questions, uses the method of re-thinking.

The different ways in which people have interpreted and responded to their circumstances is not a function of human psychology and physiology but rather a reflection of their historical experience. The world as a thing in itself is unknowable; it can only be known and interpreted through theories and ideas. A world view allows the raw data of experience to be interpreted and understood. All world views involve the interpretation of experience. When a people have shared a common historical experience there emerges a group world view of 'reality' in which there is strong agreement about the meaning of specific events and phenomena. These world views, however, are not static but change as new ideas become accepted or new problems are identified. An account of such changes with geographical ramifications and how they occur is the essential task of the historical geographer.

Historical change is dialectical.[13] The world is always interpreted from a specific point of view, which at any given moment is a legacy of the past. The reality of the present is a creation of the historical past, because this past provides the ideas on which the world is interpreted. If we wish to understand the twentieth century we must understand the societies of the nineteenth century from which modern society developed. The nineteenth century must, in turn, be understood in relation to the historical legacy of the period preceding it, and so on backwards through time. The objective of historical geography is to understand historical change, but such change never takes place in a vacuum of ideas. Indeed, the impossibility of understanding con-temporary ideas, except historically, makes the study of history important in all fields of human endeavour.

There is no logical basis for differentiating historical geography from history. Although historians have tended to concern themselves with political and social questions, geographers with human settlement and the use of the land, these differences, to the extent that they are empirically valid, are of no philosophical importance. The fact that many historical geographers (that is, scholars doing historical geography) are found within departments of geography is justified, if at all, on pragmatic grounds. A historical geographer with a background in, for example, climatology, plant geography and soils is probably in a better position to evaluate and understand human activity on the land than someone without such knowledge, although he must be careful not to assume that the people he investigates have the same knowledge as he has.

If all history is the history of thought, all historical geography is the history of thought relating to human activity on the land. The thought of interest to historical geographers will include more than ideas about the natural environment. The way different peoples have evaluated their environments is but one of many elements shaping the character of geographical activity. The ideas of Sauer and Wright that one should look at the natural environment from the perspective of the people one is studying must be extended to include political, economic and social ideas.

An actual historical geographical analysis will seek to elucidate the meaning of human activity on the earth by treating such activity as expressions of human purposes. Although such elucidation will be related to thought, an analysis will not always be primarily concerned with re-thinking particular decisions. Rather, the aim might be to draw out some general implications of individual or group purposes. For example one might analyse the ramifications of housing policies in relation to the kinds of developments encouraged or discouraged by them. One might then ask whether or not these developments were in accordance with the purposes of the policy. If not, why not?

Question and answer

There is a widely held belief that empirical investigations will yield little of interest unless informed by theory. This view is rejected, without accepting that the alternative to theoretical approaches is a lifeless narrative of events. The essence of history does not depend on theory but on questions. The facts of the past will not tell a historian what he wants to know until he questions them. Historical knowledge cannot, therefore, be obtained simply by collecting and ordering facts. The past must be approached with questions. In asking a question the historian seeks to discover the meaning that a fact or series of facts had in the unique situation in which they were imbedded.

An important aspect of Collingwood's philosophy of history was based upon his 'logic of question and answer'.[14] He conceived of historical investigation in terms of question-and-answer complexes. In such a complex each question and each answer had to 'belong'. The questions asked would 'arise' out of one's investigation; the answers would be 'right' if they led to further questions.

The application of this question-and-answer method is illustrated in Collingwood's archaeological work on the Roman wall between the Tyne and Solway. (Collingwood seems to have had a particular passion for the study of walls.) Until Collingwood took another look, archaeologists had conceived of the wall as a frontier defense without asking how the wall performed its function. In asking this question Collingwood came to the conclusion that it was an 'elevated sentry walk' rather than a traditional defensive wall.[15] This answer immediately gave rise to an additional question. If the Tyne–Solway structure was used for surveillance, a (new) question arose as to the provisions the Romans had made for watching the sea approaches to this area. The posing of this question led to the search for additional structures of surveillance, and resulted in the discovery of a series of watchtowers along the coast.[16]

Collingwood was convinced that successful excavation in archaeology depended on formulating good questions. The questions arose out of the work already done, and would frequently be related to problems of interpretation. Collingwood took pains to argue against the empirically oriented scholars, who made a career of collecting facts unrelated to historical questions.[17] The empirical approach within an idealist framework is not a mindless search for facts, although it is not directly informed by scientific theories.

The historian is concerned with human actions as expressions of intentions and purposes. This concern can be a guide in all kinds of historical investigation, no matter what the character of the historical record. It is no paradox that Collingwood's historical research lay in a historical field which was wanting in written documents. The idea of re-enactment is as valid for archaeological research as it is for documentary research. The fundamental difference between an archaeologist and a palaeontologist is that the latter looks at his 'finds' as a means for uncovering the thoughts they express. The archaeologist must ask: 'What was the purpose of this ditch? How was it intended to work? Did it work as it was supposed to work'?[18] Such questions cannot be asked by a palaeontologist about trilobites.

Objectivity

It is common to think of science as objective, and to regard other approaches to explanation and understanding as subjective. The claim of science to objectivity rests on the availability of well-confirmed laws. Where such laws are lacking there can be no guarantee of objectivity. The notion that other approaches to explanation are subjective is only valid to the extent that one accepts the scientific definition of objectivity. It will be argued here that idealist or rational understanding is in principle capable of being objective in the ordinary meaning of this word. In ascribing a particular calculation to a geographical or historical agent as an explanation of his actions a scholar either ascribes a true calculation or a false one. A correct interpretation of why agent A took action X will be one in which the thought ascribed to A for doing X is consistent with all the available evidence. If the assumption that actions are products of rational calculation is accepted, it seems logical to claim that a correct understanding of an action is obtained when the thought contained in it is re-enacted and comprehended in the scholar's mind.

The recognition that there exists, in principle, a correct interpretation of a specific action is one issue; to know whether the interpretation actually put forward is the correct one is quite another. One can never be certain that one has understood a historical geographical situation correctly. Historical understanding aspires to be objective not on a basis of certainty, but on the elaboration of general rules or criteria against which candidate interpretations can be assessed. In all cases these rules demand that an interpretation be supported with appropriate empirical evidence that is open to public scrutiny. In many situations lack of adequate data must prevent a final judgement on the merits of competing interpretations. In others, competing interpretations might have strengths and weaknesses which makes a choice among them difficult. If the idea of historical geography as a critical endeavour exists, and if scholars commit themselves to the discovery of all the relevant evidence that might be brought to bear on a case, the possibility of correctly interpreting past actions would appear to exist. But no one can guarantee error-free study.

In a criticism of the re-thinking approach, Watts and Watts question whether objective interpretations are possible.[19] They suggest that I might have been misled by the available evidence in concluding that Columbus sought to reach China by sailing westwards when, in fact, he knew of America's existence all along but kept it secret for personal reasons. This example, however, far from negating the importance of re-enacting thought confirms its value, because both the original interpretation and the proposed alternative depend on making inferences about the mind of Columbus. The preferred interpretation in this case, as in others, will be the one that is most convincingly related to the available evidence. I would submit that a strong case can be made for the accidental discovery of the New World by Columbus; but, of course, the evidence will never be conclusive beyond a shadow of a doubt. If conclusive proof of this case is required, a criterion of perfection is demanded which eliminates not only the idealist but everyone else as well.

The concept of a correct understanding, which was developed with respect to a specific individual action, can be broadened to apply to the collective behaviour of groups. The inability of those seeking to understand human activity to identify every single thought involved in a specific situation is not a valid argument against the possibility of understanding it. An acceptable interpretation will be one that correctly identifies the general factors behind a movement. For example, an explanation of why European settlers moved onto the frontier in North America would involve setting down (with supporting evidence) those factors which were responsible for the migrants' actions. The fact that one cannot produce the identical thought patterns of the human agents of geographical change is less crucial than one's being able, in re-enacting their thought, to identify the meaning that specific phenomena had for specific individuals and groups in the appropriate social context. In this respect again the historical geographer is not in a very different position from a physicist who, in describing a unique experiment, is only expected to include the conditions and laws pertinent to its outcome.

Although a historian, like scientists, must use his imagination in seeking to provide accurate accounts of his subject, his task is quite different from that of the novelist. Collingwood has described the basic differences.

As works of imagination, the historian's work and the novelist's do not differ. Where they do differ is that the historian's picture is meant to be true. The novelist has a single task only: to construct a coherent picture, one that makes sense. The historian has a double task: he has both to do this, and to construct a picture of things as they really were and of events as they really happened. This further necessity imposes upon him obedience to three rules of method, from which the novelist or artist in general is free.[20]

Collingwood elaborates on three rules of method for the historian. Firstly, the historian must localize his account in time and space. Secondly, all history must be consistent with itself. And thirdly, the historian's account must be based on evidence that is available to general scrutiny and assessment. These rules are designed to ensure against history as pure invention or propaganda. They make possible critical debate among historians as to the merits of specific historical interpretations.

The possibility of approaching a given area or topic from many different perspectives is not an argument against the possibility of objective historical geography. If one scholar for personal reasons seeks to explain the farming activities of large land holders in a certain country, while another concentrates his attention on peasant producers, there is no reason the two studies should conflict with one another. Indeed, if both scholars were equally assiduous in seeking to understand the relevant thoughts involved in the geographic activities of their subjects, one would expect the studies to complement each other. The fact that all studies have points of view is not synonymous with bias, although an interest in a particular group can lead to bias if the scholar identifies himself emotionally with it.

The imaginative re-creation of the thought of individuals and groups expressed in their geographical activity provides the foundation of an explicitly historical human geography. This approach permits the scholar to evaluate the meaning of actions in terms of their significance for a society. In other words, historical actions of geographical significance are identified as those actions that have some bearing on understanding the changing relationships of a society in its physical environment. The historical geographer identifies such actions by re-thinking the thoughts of his subjects in their social and cultural context. In theory, then, a single objective historical geography could accurately reconstruct the critical or historic episodes in the society's settlement and occupancy of an area. A historic action is not historic merely because certain historians might have labelled it as such, but rather because it can be shown to have shaped the way people relate to each other and the world around them.

The idea of producing objective historical geographical work is not so much a 'noble dream', but an essential goal of scholarly activity. Historical geographical research, like other scholarly activity, is premised on the idea of cooperation among its practitioners. Such cooperation is scarcely possible if individual geographers do not share broadly similar ideas about what it is that historical geographers are seeking to accomplish. The past as such does not provide an adequate basis for bringing together a group of scholars, because the past, as I have shown, encompasses all the disciplines. A coherent history or historical geography can only be built upon an acceptance of a criterion of historical meaning. The past is, thereby, shrunk into a more manageable historic past. The importance of thought in human actions is largely in providing just such a criterion.

Although the idea of objectivity is considered of vital importance in scholarly work, the goal itself is never likely to be reached. The historians themselves are not operating in a vacuum, but as members of living societies, and their writing will reflect this inescapable fact. In short, the historian will create a past which will inevitably be shaped by the historian's own position in a society having specific ideas and beliefs. There are precautions that can be taken against the cruder forms of misrepresentation. A historian will need to be on constant guard not to impute to historical figures the world view of his own society, or imagine that currently accepted categories have universal validity.

Yet even those historians who manage to avoid more obvious problems relating to the interpretation of evidence will not be able to claim their accounts are final. Collingwood has identified the reasons for this situation.

The evidence available for solving any given problem changes with every change of historical method and with every variation in the competence of historians. The principles by which this evidence is interpreted change too since the interpreting of evidence is a task to which a man must bring everything he knows: historical knowledge, knowledge of nature and man, mathematical knowledge, philosophical knowledge; and not knowledge only, but mental habits and possessions of every kind: and none of these is unchanging. Because of these changes, which never cease, however slow they may appear to observers who take a short view, every new generation must rewrite history in its own way.[21]

Although a final definitive history may not be possible, Collingwood makes it clear that this is not an argument for historical scepticism. He writes:

It is only the discovery of a second dimension of historical thought, the history of history: the discovery that the historian himself, together with the here-and-now which forms the total body of evidence available to him, is a part of the process he is studying, has his own place in that process, and can see it only from the point of view which at this present moment he occupies within it.[22]

The idea that historical experiences are those experiences having a significant or lasting impact on the mind provides a foundation for more focused historical geographical studies. A major shortcoming of many contemporary studies in historical fields is that it is difficult to see exactly how such studies contribute to understanding the larger picture. This criticism applies with its greatest force to those studies whose aim is to illustrate or test theoretical propositions. The adoption of an idealist philosophy would provide a criterion of historical significance. It would encourage historical geographers to approach the past from a similar point of view, and would stimulate debate about the precise historical importance of specific experiences and events. Such debate would encourage more detailed investigations of specific problems with a view to settling points of contention.

Conclusion

The view that the re-enactment of the thought in actions is a useful mode of historical analysis, but is hardly the foundation of an independent concept of history, misses the essential point of the idealist position. The words 'all history is the history of thought' describe in a nutshell the essence of the philosophy of history presented here. Those critics who point out that physical and psychological elements are ignored (in the conviction that this represents a grave shortcoming of the approach) have explicitly or implicitly embraced the natural-scientific concept of history in which a good explanation is synonymous with providing an account of the necessary and sufficient conditions for the occurrence of a phenomenon. History begins with human thought, and natural phenomena only become of historical interest because of human appraisals. If the earth were destroyed by a meteor it would not be an event of history, although it would end the possibility of history. In limiting historical geography to thought one establishes a criterion of historicity. This conception provides a basis for the objective study of the past, because it implies a criterion against which the historical significance of geographical phenomena can be evaluated. A phenomenon cannot qualify as being of historical significance unless it is somehow made part of human consciousness. The precise significance a phenomenon acquires is, in turn, a function of how it is construed by the historical mind.

References and notes

1 R. G. Collingwood. *The idea of history* (New York, Oxford University Press, 1956), p. 215.
2 R. G. Collingwood and J. N. L. Myers, *Roman Britain and the English settlements* (London, Oxford University Press, 1937), pp. 124–34.
3 L. J. Goldstein, 'Collingwood's theory of historical knowing', *History and Theory*, **9** (1970), 32.
4 Collingwood, *Idea*, p. 200.
5 *Ibid.*, p. 214.

54   *Objections to rational understanding*

6 *Ibid.*
7 *Ibid.*
8 L. O. Mink, *Mind, history and dialectic the philosophy of R. G. Collingwood* (Bloomington, Indiana University Press, 1969), p. 172.
9 See Mink, *Mind*, pp. 162–70 for an extended discussion of this point.
10 R. C. Harris, 'Theory and synthesis in historical geography', *The Canadian Geographer*, **15** (1971), 167.
11 See Mink, *Mind*, pp. 82–92.
12 Collingwood, *Idea*, p. 227.
13 L. Rubinoff, *Collingwood and the reform of metaphysics* (Toronto, University of Toronto Press, 1970), p. 228.
14 R. G. Collingwood, *An Autobiography* (Oxford, Oxford University Press, 1938), p. 29–43.
15 *Ibid.*, pp. 128–9.
16 *Ibid.*, p. 129.
17 *Ibid.*, pp. 124–6.
18 *Ibid.*, p. 128.
19 S. J. Watts and S. J. Watts, 'On the idealist alternative in geography and history', *The Professional Geographer,* **30** (1978), 123–7. See also R. T. Harrison and D. N. Livingstone, 'There and back again – towards a critique of idealist human geography', *Area,* **11** (1979), 75–8 for a critique of the idealist position.
20 Collingwood, *Idea*, p. 246.
21 *Ibid.*, p. 248.
22 *Ibid.*

4

Historical Geography as science

Is history a science? This question is the subject of continuing debate in the philosophy of history and has yet to be finally answered. Although a similar question was often asked by geographers, it seems to have created far less controversy. Hartshorne probably had general support among geographers when he rephrased this question to read 'What kind of science is geography?'[1] The question, 'Is historical geography a science?' is still worth asking, however, because it raises basic questions about the objectives and nature of historical enquiry.

The word 'science' can be defined in various ways. A definition of science as a body of organized knowledge presents no difficulties. On this definition practically all knowledge that is based on systematic principles can be regarded as scientific. The use of a broad definition of science, however, begs the question. In asking whether history is a science one is generally concerned about whether historical explanations involve the use of theories and laws. There are a number of ways in which history can be conceived of as science in this sense, including an important Marxist variant.

The crux of the case for history as science rests on how one conceives of a historical explanation. The advocates of the scientific view of history argue that historical explanations have the same form as natural-scientific ones. By this view, the essence of science is not a procedure or method, but a mode of explanation dependent on laws and theories. Following Hempel, a scientific explanation is conceived of as a deductive argument of the form

$$C_1, C_2, \ldots, C_k \qquad \text{Explanans}$$

$$\underline{L_1, L_2, \ldots, L_r}$$

$$E \qquad \text{Explanandum sentence}$$

Here, $C_1, C_2, \ldots, C_k$ are sentences describing the determining or (initial) conditions or the particular circumstances existing before the occurrence of E, the event to be explained, and $L_1, L_2, \ldots, L_r$ are the general laws on which the explanation of E rests.[2] The occurrence of event E is the logical outcome of the situation described in the *explanans*. This form of explanation is known as deductive–nomological explanation. The model is dependent for its power on the existence of general laws, which must be true and reasonably well confirmed by empirical evidence.

On the basis of deductive–nomological explanation historical geography can be conceived of as either an essentially law-using science or as an essentially law-seeking (theoretical) one. Each of these possibilities needs to be examined.

Laws and historical understanding

The complexity of factors involved in the historical development of human societies means that every individual place or region is unique in the sense that it differs from all others in some respects. This uniqueness is often put forward as an argument against the possibility of deductive–nomological explanation. Uniqueness itself, however, does not provide a basis on which history is separate from science. Hempel and Oppenheim have pointed out that 'every individual event, in the physical sciences no less than in psychology or the social sciences, is unique in the sense that it, with all its particular characteristics, does not repeat itself'.[3] Although the uniqueness involved in a physical experiment might be of a trivial kind such as the colour of the experimenter's tie, the mere fact that it can be considered trivial is based upon deductive–nomological understanding. An evidently simple laboratory experiment would be indescribably complex if someone attempted to provide a complete account of every element.

The closest parallels to history in the physical sciences are law-using disciplines like meteorology and geology. In these disciplines the possibility of experimental work is strictly limited and individual phenomena are often exceedingly complex. Nevertheless, both meteorology and geology are properly considered sciences, and their practitioners use a deductive–nomological model of explanation. The laws on which their explanations are based, however, are the laws of physics, chemistry and other sciences. In other words, meteorology and geology can be conceived of as essentially law-applying sciences rather than as law-seeking ones. There is absolutely no reason why historical geography should not be regarded, like meteorology or geology, as a law-applying science. The insistence on the universal applicability of the deductive–nomological model of scientific explanation does not mean that each discipline will have its own independent laws and theories.

The concept of historical geography as a law-applying or law-consuming science, however, does involve problems of implementation. In the case of meteorology and geology, a large number of well-confirmed physical and other laws are available to be used. This situation does not exist in historical disciplines; a critical issue of scientific history or historical geography concerns the availability of general laws, which have some empirical foundation. Laws cannot perform their basic function in scientific explanations if strict criteria of empirical verification or confirmation are not applied to them. The success of physics and chemistry and disciplines based upon them is largely attributable to rigorous tests given to hypotheses and theories before accepting them as laws. A nonprobabilistic law, because it defines a necessary connection between events, can be refuted by a single well-confirmed negative result. Probabilistic laws might need a series of negative results, but such laws must be formulated precisely enough to be testable and refutable if they are to be given a meaningful role in scientific explanation.[4]

The general requirement for the acceptance of a scientific law is that it successfully pass empirical tests that are replicable by other workers, and are therefore open to independent confirmation. In philosophical terms any law or theory which seeks to acquire scientific status must, in principle, be testable and refutable.[5] This criterion of acceptability makes no mention of intuitive understanding, and assumes that a causal connection cannot be inferred from the nature of reality or from common-sense expectations. For example, the only valid scientific reason for rejecting astrological 'laws' is the failure of such laws when subjected to genuine empirical tests. The apparently preposterous idea that the position of the stars might influence human behaviour by itself provides no logical grounds for rejecting astrology. The rejection of intuition as a basis on which laws and theories might be accepted makes it all the more necessary for science to insist upon rigorous empirical tests for candidate laws and theories, because, without such tests, there would be no *logical* basis for the exclusion from science of witchcraft, astrology, or any other bogus theory.

The scientific approach, therefore, requires laws capable of meeting minimum criteria of scientific acceptability. Anyone who argues that the criteria of acceptability for laws and theories are too strict must face the problem of establishing weaker criteria for inclusion of certain propositions which would not, at the same time, permit the inclusion of inadequate laws from areas such as astrology or environmental determinism. The criteria for the scientific acceptance of laws must be stringent enough to exclude untestable laws and accidental generalizations. This condition means that the criteria of universality upon which philosophers of science insist cannot be relaxed without unacceptable consequences.

Hempel espoused a unified science which included history.[6] He recognized that historical explanations lacked the precision of explanations in sciences like physics or biology, but he argued that such explanations nevertheless depended on laws. Hempel referred to historical explanations as 'explanation sketches', because they were loosely formulated and the laws on which they rested were seldom made explicit. From a logical point of view the role of laws in historical explanation is no less crucial than in any other science. Although Hempel's position implied that historical explanations would be improved if they rested on laws which were formulated with more precision, he did not advocate a radical change in the style of historical enquiry. His main purpose was merely to show that history contained the essential elements of a scientific discipline.

The concept of law-applying science is much more applicable to the basic objectives of historical geography than the concept of a law-seeking one, yet the notion of history as a law-applying science is not immune to criticism. Dray argued that a typical historical account of an event did not commit a historian to the deductive–nomological model of explanation. Any laws that were essential ingredients of historical explanation, he maintained, were either so general or trivial as to have no explanatory power or they were so specific as to apply to a single case.[7] Such laws might be logically necessary, but, Dray concluded, they were methodologically unimportant because they added nothing to one's understanding of a situation.

In spite of reformulations which emphasized the importance of probabilistic laws, the deductive–nomological model of explanation was severely handicapped by the inability of its advocates to produce laws which were both precise and reasonably well confirmed by empirical evidence. Although it was comparatively easy to give certain historical explanations a deductive–nomological form, it was almost impossible to provide such explanations with solid empirical content, because of a lack of general laws of human behaviour.

The poverty of laws describing human actions is sometimes explained by appealing to the undeveloped state of social science, but there are several arguments which suggest that the problem of finding laws of human behaviour may be of a more fundamental kind. One of these arguments points out that later events involving human beings can be influenced by earlier ones in novel ways, similar situations leading to very different results. For example, the men who made the Russian Revolution were influenced by the French Revolution and the Paris Commune. Carr argued that Stalin came to power because certain Bolshevik leaders, fearing that Trotsky might become another Napoleon, gave Stalin their support at a crucial moment in the power struggle that followed Lenin's death.[8] Another argument points out that man follows conventions of his own creation which vary from place to place and from time to time. Any 'law' of human behaviour that might be discovered would be limited to a particular society. Notwithstanding these and other objections, many philosophers of science, although admitting that no social laws have yet been found, retain a cautious optimism. Ernest Nagel, for instance, had argued that social scientists must continue to search for laws, because a belief that laws cannot be found will certainly ensure that they will not be found – even if they actually do exist.[9]

Yet even if some laws pertaining to human society were to be discovered, the essential problems of historical geography would not be solved. The basic task of a historical geographer is to provide a coherent account of change in unique historical contexts. The historical geographer is concerned with the meaning of human actions rather than their causes; the social scientist is concerned with such actions as instances of theories or laws. Historical fields are not and never can be applied social science, because the concrete circumstances of a situation provide the criterion of historical meaning. For example, a social scientist might understand a riot in terms of the psychology of crowds; the historian's interest in the same event would focus on the meaning of the riot in the social context in which it occurred.

Theoretical approaches

Although historical understanding would appear to have different objectives from those of social science, historical geography is sometimes conceived of as a social-scientific endeavour (as opposed to an endeavour making use of the results of social sciences). The advocates of such a position see geographers becoming actively involved in the development of theory and laws to explain human geographical activity. Although it is recognized that the complexity of human forms of life might make it difficult to formulate universal theories, there are procedures that can be used to overcome such difficulties. One such procedure is the development of theoretical models, in which the scholar deliberately reduces the complexity of the real world to a more manageable 'ideal' world. The role of such models in geographical understanding has been frequently misconstrued.

Theoretical models are aids to understanding, no more and no less. In the simplified situation postulated by a model it is possible to acquire a clearer grasp of how a few variables interact in a given situation. Such understanding, however, usually depends on rational principles, not laws. In the Von Thünen model of agricultural activity in an isolated state, for example, the foundation of understanding derives from our ability (and this is the crucial point) to re-think or re-calculate the thought behind the specific actions of farmers at various distances from the market centre. In other words, models of the Von Thünen type would lack credibility were it not for the user's ability to see a rational connection between a farmer's crop emphasis and the farmer's situation. The plausibility of the model is not derived from laws but from assumptions of rationality imputed to the hypothetical inhabitants of the isolated state by Von Thünen. These models are recognized as potentially valuable in helping to understand more complex real-world situations, because they demonstrate the logical outcomes of specific assumptions.

Models have no logical role to play in the explanation of the real world, however, and any attempt to use them in this way or to test them must be regarded as a misconstrual of their logical character. No explanatory inferences can be based on the model, even if actual conditions resemble those postulated. For example, the discovery of agricultural rings around an isolated city would not give one grounds for assuming that the people were behaving in the same manner as Von Thünen's farmers. A careful investigation might find that the people in question were in fact in a similar situation to the farmers of Von Thünen's isolated state, but one's explanation would still stand or fall on its own. Before a model such as Von Thünen's could be given any explanatory power it would have to be set out in a form, 'under conditions 1, 2, 3, isolated cities spawn specialized rings of agriculture . . . *x, y, z*.' This proposition would then have to be tested on isolated cities conforming to the specified limits. Only if it successfully passed several tests would one be justified in elevating the proposition to the status of a law, and then, and only then, could it be accorded explanatory power in real situations.

In spite of logical difficulties many geographers have sought to explain real-world phenomena with the help of abstract models based on simplified assumptions about human behaviour. The lack of correspondence between reality and a model is easily explained away by showing that certain assumptions of the model have been violated in reality. Such explanations rest on the (dubious) assumption that the logical structure of a model guarantees its empirical validity. The purpose of empirical research, however, is to test hypotheses, models and theories, and testing in science is only valid where failure is possible. The well-known models of Von Thünen, Christaller and Lösch all lack empirical support, and, therefore, are of no help in the explanation of the real world. I do not say these models have no value. Abstract models based on simplified assumptions about reality can be useful, but only if they are recognized for what they are, namely abstractions without empirical status.

A historical geographer almost denies history when he seeks to understand historical situations solely in terms of models. In the first place, the creator of a model often assumes that 'ideal' conditions apply, and drastically simplifies the complexities of real-world situations. This procedure is essentially antihistorical because it denies the complexity created by history itself. In historical geography the world is not a *tabula rasa*, but a complex entity created from past events. In the second place, models assume that change is a process in which 'all other things are equal', yet the essence of historical development is that 'all other things are *not* equal'. Few processes, based upon fixed or predictable relationships among phenomena, are allowed to 'run their course'. The problem of creating models of historical development has led some scientifically minded historians to look at history as a predictable process that is from time to time interrupted by unpredictable 'chance' events. Such a conception, however, creates an arbitrary distinction among historical events which is imposed on the past by the historian and not discovered in the events themselves.[10]

The failure of the scientific approach in human geography is manifest in the debate over whether an investigator is inevitably biased by his theories. The idea that theories could be a source of bias would be unthinkable in a discipline based on genuine scientific principles, yet in history and the social sciences the lack of objective tests for theories makes the charge that general theory creates bias less absurd than it would otherwise be. Hempel said that a major objective of physical science is the improvement of mankind's control or strategic advantage over Nature.[11] In human studies untestable theories become ideologies, whose implementation benefits some groups more than others. The advocates of *laissez-faire*, for example, use theory as a weapon for securing strategic advantage over their opponents. Such theory is, of course, unscientific because it is formulated in such a way as to be incapable of failing an empirical test.

Marxism

The idea that a theory must be capable of meeting objective tests applies to all theories, including Marx's historical materialism. The problem here is to identify the theory one is supposed to test. A wide variety of different positions can be considered historical materialist or Marxist.[12] In a brief discussion it is not possible to explicate the complex character of Marx's historical materialist ideas in any depth, but is is possible to identify three basic approaches, each of which poses distinct problems. For convenience, they are identified as (1) 'weak' (or flexible); (2) 'original', and (3) 'revisionist'.

In the 'weak' formulation of historical materialism the economic structure of society created out of the forces of production is considered to be the most important influence on its historical development, but this influence is not regarded as a deterministic one to the exclusion of other factors. The forces of production shaping the development of society will be greatly modified by legal, political, and social conditions. This position loses much of its power in admitting that the forces of production can be modified and changed by other factors.

Most scholars, including historical geographers, examine a wide range of factors that might help to explain concrete historical situations. The acknowledgement that economic factors, modes of production, and class relationships might be of importance to historical understanding does not necessarily make one a Marxist, any more than the recognition that environmental factors could be significant in certain situations makes one an environmental determinist. Whether a particular study in which economic factors predominate, but not to the exclusion of others, is classified as Marxist would appear to be a question of minor importance. The key point is the open-mindedness that a historical geographer brings to empirical evidence. An avowedly Marxian, but open-minded, empirical analysis would probably differ little from an idealist one.

A good example of an empirical Marxist approach is *The making of the English working class* by E. P. Thompson.[13] The Marxist orientation of the author is reflected partly in the topic he has selected and partly in his sympathetic treatment of it. Yet Thompson takes evidence seriously and he does not seek to impose a rigid theoretical structure on his material. In emphasizing that man makes himself and that the English working class participated in its own creation, Thompson adopts a view of historical process that is entirely compatible with an idealist position. The crucial issue here is not so much the nature of a historian's presuppositions, but rather his willingness to develop an interpretation on the basis of empirical evidence.

A corollary of the notion that human beings make their own history is the rejection of theory in historical explanation. What people have made of themselves is a historical question that must be answered empirically, not theoretically. Either humans have made themselves or they have been made by their (total) environment. If the former, the emphasis of historical research must be on mind and what it has made of itself in different situations. If the latter, mind becomes a mere reflection of objective conditions, and theoretical approaches are not only justified but absolutely necessary. I do not see any way in which these two approaches can be combined at a philosophical level without creating insoluble problems.

Marxism in its original formulation has more teeth, and is a general theory of historical change in which relationships among classes provide a basis for the prediction of future states of society. The original writings of Marx contain a number of predictions that have not been borne out by events. Any theory which fails crucial empirical tests is invalidated from a scientific point of view. The original formulation of Marxist theory is clearly false. When Marxism is advocated as an alternative philosophy we can assume that it is not the original thesis that is being put forward, but rather some modification of it.

The task of modern Marxist scholarship might be construed as the extension of the original historical materialist thesis. In this view, Marx becomes a foundation on which theories applicable to real societies are to be constructed. This view would seem to have elements in common with positivist historical geography. The positivist would probably maintain that, although laws capable of meeting stringent scientific tests have yet to be formulated, such laws do, in fact, exist to be discovered. The historical materialist has his own ideas about what the laws of society would look like, but like the positivist would maintain that such laws do exist and must be 'discovered'.

Although it is not possible to predict the future course of scholarship, it is possible to set down criteria against which certain kinds of scholarship should be assessed. Any interpretation that is based on general relationships or laws must be testable and refutable. Marxist theory, in common with other general theories that would claim explanatory power, must be formulated in a manner which permits it to be tested.

A proposition such as 'the history of all hitherto existing societies is the history of class struggle' raises immediate difficulties. If one interprets this statement using a rigid definition of class it poses immediate difficulties of empirical verification. If one gives the proposition a loose meaning it becomes so porous it is virtually impossible to refute. Any empirical data are open to interpretation in these terms if the scholar introduces notions such as 'hidden struggles' and is allowed to make use of other ad-hoc hypotheses. However, once a proposition becomes incapable of failing empirical tests it loses its explanatory power.

The stronger the claims of a theory and the weaker the evidence in its support the more it needs built-in theoretical devices to protect it from refutation. A protective clause permits a scholar to discount evidence that would, if accepted at its face value, place his theory in jeopardy. The rigid structuralist interpretation of Marx has been formulated complete with its 'protective devices'. In this case one of the 'protective devices' is 'determination in the last instance'.[14] This clause permits any number of linkages to be established between a material cause and its final effect. 'Determination in the last instance' is not determination at all, but an 'unhappy mongrel' reminiscent of Taylor's 'stop and go' environmental determinism.[15]

Historical materialism, in common with many theories, cannot be given scientific status on the basis of its empirical success. This failure might not be crucial if historical materialism is construed as a philosophy rather than a scientific theory. As a philosophy its key propositions would be accepted before any empirical evidence was collected, and the objective of research would not be to test the truth of the thesis but rather to illustrate its truth. Its propositions would no longer be in the realm of science, but in the realm of belief or faith. This attribute renders Marxist theory unsuitable as a general framework of knowledge in historical geography. Lack of empirical support would not negate the political objectives of Marxism. As an ideology, historical materialism performs a purpose in providing a viewpoint on the political process. This type of theoretical perspective might make for good politics, but it is bad scholarship.

The case Harvey makes against objective science in *Social justice and the city* is an example of the distortions that Marxian premises can create. Harvey argued that the growth of natural science should be interpreted in relation to its materialistic basis, and he noted that 'material activity involves the manipulation of nature in the interests of man, and scientific understanding cannot be interpreted independently of that general thrust'.[16] This premise is given a more precise focus. Harvey maintained that one would expect natural science in the West 'to reflect a drive for manipulation and control over those aspects of nature that are relevant to the middle class'.[17] The third step in the argument leads Harvey to conclude that revolutions of thought in the natural sciences 'pose no threat to the existing order since they are constructed with the requirements of that existing order broadly in mind'.[18] Although there is some truth in Harvey's assertions in relation to what might be termed 'science' policy (focusing on applied science and technology), the general thrust of Harvey's case is simply an incredible misinterpretation of the history of science.

The founders of modern science (although not always applying their knowledge in practical matters) were as often as not at odds with the established order, not so much because they were actively seeking this role (many tried to avoid confrontation), but because their quest for knowledge made such confrontations almost inevitable. When Galileo argued for the Copernican theory, the last thing on his mind seems to have been 'the requirement of the existing order'. Is it really accurate to claim that people like Pasteur, Darwin and Einstein constructed theories with the 'existing order broadly in mind'? The suggestion that natural scientists are representatives of the middle class interpreting the natural world in ways that will be politically acceptable is preposterous. When scientists propose theories their first objective must be to produce an account of Nature that fits the facts. This necessity has fortunately been recognized by many scientists, who have devised elaborate procedures to ensure that new ideas are open to proper (objective) verification. It is virtually impossible for a scientist in struggling with a problem to keep anything in mind, except the requirements of a satisfactory theory. Although a successful theory will often have practical implications, these implications are often impossible to predict and are as likely as not to be unsettling to the established order.

The status of knowledge in the social sciences poses difficulties which are not so easily dealt with. Social and economic theories are often based on assumptions about society which, if implemented, tend to favour certain groups. Not surprisingly, specific groups and classes within a society have adopted theories of social change most likely to advance their causes successfully. Self-interested theory has nothing to do with science, because the adherents of such theory seldom feel obliged to alter their views in the face of negative evidence. When a theory serves a political purpose it is best construed as an ideology without scientific status. Harvey's notion that theory can be classified as revolutionary or counter-revolutionary replaces *objective* criteria of theory acceptance with *political* ones.

One need not follow Harvey to this point. If it is insisted that all social science theories must, like any theory in science, be capable of being refuted, a criterion is established which is capable of eliminating any theory that does not 'square' with empirical evidence. Such a criterion, when properly applied, will be blind to the political implications of a theory, and eliminate the idea that there might be such categories as 'revolutionary' and 'counter-revolutionary' theory, however one cares to define these terms. In the final analysis, Harvey's idea that a theory must meet a political criterion of acceptability is dangerous, not because it poses a threat to the established society, but because, if accepted, it would eliminate the idea of truth from scholarship and sound the death knell of free enquiry.

The notion that history exhibits some general pattern or is propelled by underlying mechanisms that cut across different societies is not new. There are, among others, cyclical theories of history, Toynbee's challenge and response thesis, and Marx's historical materialism. None of these theories seems to provide a convincing explanation of the wide variety of societies in the real world. I prefer to approach the study of history on a case-by-case basis eschewing a commitment to general statements about all societies. This procedure seems likely to ensure a more objective account of 'what really happened', precisely because it is uncommitted to general theory.

It should not be necessary to go into more detail on the extent to which an enquiry based on a commitment to an untestable theory can *distort the truth*. If Harvey's interpretation of the nature of physical science is an example of a committed explanation, the fewer such explanations we have (in geography) the better. The acceptance, in principle, of the notion of committed explanations would open the door to every conceivable kind of explanation as people with commitments to their particular cause re-interpreted the past. The ideal should rather be to the uncommitted explanation. If it can be shown that explanations in historical geography have been distorted by middle-class assumptions, the answer is to eliminate the assumptions that generated the distortion, not to create new distortions favouring other groups.

Nevertheless, the charge by Marxist geographers that many human geographers, who accept the underlying ideas of capitalism, have used theory to support the capitalist state is essentially correct. When Marxists offer (geographers) a choice of either supporting capitalism or helping to tear it down, they display theoretical bias of their own. To get off the horns of this dilemma one has only to insist that *all* theories which claim scientific status must successfully pass objective tests. I am doubtful, however, that any theory in historical geography or social science would be capable of passing such tests. The idealist concept of re-enactment provides an alternative approach to understanding, which allows one to give (in principle) objective, value-free explanations without having to resort to theories of dubious status. The idealist is also able to side-step the Marxist criticism of theoretical bias by rejecting theory of all descriptions, insisting that human conflicts be analysed from a neutral or politically uncommitted vantage point, and suggesting the way in which such investigations can be carried out.

Theoretical approaches have failed in history, and historical geography, because such approaches conceive of history as an external spectacle of change, which can be understood in a natural-scientific way. Yet if history is anything it is not a predictable ordered process. In fact, history exists precisely because whatever order it exhibits at a given time is never a final order. Human inventions and discoveries are creating new rules and relationships which by their very nature are unpredictable.

Although attempts to create a scientific history in which order is imposed by the historian have not been successful, this failure does not mean we cannot understand the past. The record of the human past is also an expression of the ideas and priorities of past societies. The historian is not required to predict what might happen, because he already knows what has happened. Before an election, we might have doubts about the popularity of a politician's election programme. The election results themselves tell us whether our doubts were justified. People express their priorities and concerns in their actions.

In addition to dealing with events that have already happened, the historian has special access to his subjects. A man cannot make a decision without thinking about what he is going to do. In looking at urbanization, for example, the historical geographer does not have to concern himself with whether people thought it worthwhile to settle in towns. He knows that the settlement took place. The only question that remains is why people moved into urban areas. He is able to answer this question by showing that for those moving to urban places it was a logical thing to do. This demonstration does not mean such action was inevitable. In many situations there is more than one logical thing to do, and because of this historians can understand actions without being able to predict them. We can follow a game of chess and understand the players' moves, but we cannot predict the course of a particular game. Historical analysis is best construed as the elucidation of meaning rather than a search for the sufficient and necessary conditions to explain the occurrence of events or actions.

Scientific methods

Although the concept of scientific history is rejected, the use of scientific techniques and methods is not. The historical geographer will use any methods that can help him reconstruct past situations and evaluate evidence. In this undertaking quantitative and statistical methods have an important role to play in discovering 'what really happened'.

A historical geographer might be interested in the rate at which frontier regions were settled, and the age composition of a frontier population. A series of statistical tables and associations might well be needed to describe what 'actually happened' as accurately as possible. In Collingwood's terminology, one would here be concerned with the 'outside of events'. In making use of statistical procedures the geographer is able to avoid the error of what might be termed 'nonexplanation', that is seeking an explanation of a state of affairs that did not in fact ever exist. The use of statistical methods in the analysis of census and other data can help prevent such mistakes, by replacing assumptions about what existed with hard data.

The use of statistical procedures is not a substitute for the critical evaluation of source materials. A statistical association will only be as good as the data on which it is based. An important part of a historical analysis will generally involve checking and evaluating the accuracy of data. This task will often require using statistical procedures, in which known data are checked against data of unknown reliability. Historical geographers need to base their interpretations on an appreciation of what has happened that is as accurate as possible.

Such procedures might seem to be similar to those used in contemporary human geography, but the description of the 'outside' of human activity is the beginning of an enquiry, not the end. Historical geographical anlaysis is concerned with elucidating or explaining the meaning of the external relationships and patterns that might have been uncovered. This elucidation will be achieved not within a scientific model of deductive–nomological explanation, but in terms of the ideas of those one is studying. For example, if a historical geographer discovers that people were moving into one area at a faster rate than into another, he must explain this situation in terms of human decisions. Such decisions would be related to the information available to those who might have been in a position to migrate, and to the way in which this information was interpreted by peoples of different backgrounds. An understanding of the differential growth rates would be based upon re-thinking the thoughts of the people who moved.

The historical geographer, in deciding which elements of the external situation merit inclusion in his work, will be guided by the subject matter of his discipline and the scale of enquiry. He will typically be concerned with describing such things as settlement patterns, population growth and movements, economic activity in the form of crops grown, field patterns, crop yields, transportation facilities and the like. Such descriptions will not imply any theoretical structure but they will depend on a host of theories from physical science. A tentative reliance on categories taken from census materials and common sense is in order in identifying external relationships, but initial categories might have been replaced by others more appropriate to the specific situation as the investigation proceeds.

A quantitative analysis of external attributes should not overwhelm the reader with statistical tables and relationships. None of these relationships can be considered historically significant until their meaning has been made clear. The historical geographer is failing in his task if he leaves his work at the stage of description (either verbal or quantitative). Statistical material in an undigested form is, at best, raw material for use by the historical geographer. It is the task of historical analysis to elucidate the historical meaning of the past, using only those data that are relevant to this purpose.

A geographer might, for example, discover that the population density of a region varied from two to five persons per square mile. This information is of no great importance on its own. The geographer's task is to elucidate whether these differences were important or had important implications for agriculture, transportation, social organization and general economic activity. In other words, the *historical* consequences of these population data need to be elucidated before their historical significance can be assessed. A difference in population density of three persons per square mile might in some contexts be highly significant and be of only minor importance in others.

In addition to their use in describing the external aspects of a situation, statistical relationships can constitute invaluable evidence in support of idealist explanations. Statistical evidence would be presented in support of a rational interpretation of human activity in a specific context rather than in support of a law or general theory. Such evidence would depend on the context. For example, a high correlation between wheat acreages and distances from markets might be evidence that farmers took account of distance to market in deciding how much wheat to grow. Additional evidence would be needed before such an interpretation could be seriously entertained. This evidence might be in the form of letters to local newspapers in which problems of transportation were raised. The basic rule that a statistical relationship does not necessarily indicate a causal relationship needs to be observed at all times. The relationship between wheat grown and distance to market might have reflected the fact that farmers closer to the market were in a better position to get loans to finance their farming operations, and might have had little to do with transportation problems as such.

Conclusion

The idea that historical analysis should use scientific models of explanation has been widely advocated. The most plausible of these scientific interpretations conceives of history as a law-consuming empirical science. In this view, history would continue to focus on the explanation of unique situations making implicit use of 'laws' of human behaviour. Although this 'covering law' model of history is not unsympathetic to history as it is actually practised, its adoption would imply that historical fields would become more closely associated with the social sciences. This concept of historical explanation, however, fails to recognize that the basic problem of a historical analysis is not explanation as such but rather the elucidation of the meaning of human actions in specific social and cultural contexts. This kind of analysis does not depend on laws for its effectiveness. A more aggressive view of scientific history argues that historical fields should develop their own theories. The problem here is formulating such theory in a way that allows it to be properly tested. Any theory that is not, in principle, open to falsification cannot be accorded scientific status, and most theories of history, including Marxist theory, fail to meet this fundamental criterion of scientific acceptability. Even though science is not an answer to historical problems of explanation and understanding, the 'methods' of science, divorced from the philosophy of science, are potentially of great value, particularly for the historical geographer who has to deal with large numbers in studying the activities of ordinary people.

References and notes

1 R. Hartshorne, *Perspective on the nature of geography* (Chicago, Rand McNally for the Association of American Geographers, 1959), p. 170.

2 C. Hempel 'Aspects of scientific explanation', in C. Hempel, *Aspects of scientific explanation* (New York, The Free Press, 1965), p. 336.

3 *Ibid.*, p. 253.

4 K. Popper, 'Science: conjectures and refutations', in K. Popper, *Conjectures and refutations*, 2nd edn (New York, Basic Books, 1965), p. 57.

5 *Ibid.*

6 C. Hempel, 'The function of general laws in history', reprinted in P. Gardiner (ed.), *Theories of history* (Glencoe, The Free Press, 1959), pp. 344–56.

7 W. Dray, *Laws and explanation in history* (Oxford, Oxford University Press, 1957).

8 E. H. Carr, *What is history*? (Harmondsworth, Penguin Books, 1964), p. 71.

9 E. Nagel, 'Determinism in history', in W. Dray (ed.), *Philosophical analysis and history* (New York, Harper and Row, 1966), p. 382.

10 M. Oakeshott, *Experience and its modes* (Cambridge, Cambridge University Press, 1933), 126–45.

11 C. Hempel, *Philosophy of natural science* (Englewood Cliffs, N.J., Prentice Hall, 1966), p. 2.

12 See R. De Koninck, 'Le matérialisme historique en géographie', *Cahiers de Géographie du Québec*, **22** (1978), 117–22; also D. Gregory, *Ideology, science and human geography* (London, Hutchinson, 1978).

13 E. P. Thompson, *The making of the English working class*, new edn (Harmondsworth, Penguin Books, 1968).

14 This idea is advanced in L. Althusser, *For Marx* (London, Allen Lane, 1969); and L. Althusser and E. Balibar, *Reading Capital* (New York, Pantheon Books, 1970). A critique is in E. P. Thompson *The poverty of theory and other essays* (New York and London, Monthly Review Press, 1978), pp. 94–8.

15 G. Taylor 'Introduction' in G. Taylor (ed.) *Geography in the twentieth century*, 3rd edn. (London, Methuen, 1957), pp. 11–16.

16 D. Harvey, *Social justice and the city* (London, Edward Arnold, 1973), p. 122.

17 *Ibid.*

18 *Ibid.*, p. 127.

5

Idealist Historical Geography: an example

An exposition of philosophical and methodological ideas is incomplete without examples of how an approach might be translated into action. This problem is particularly important in the case of idealist analysis, because many historical studies of geographical or economic activity do not treat human decision-making explicitly. The main defining characteristic of an idealist analysis is not whether thought is given explicit recognition (this will largely depend on the subject matter) but whether human actions are understood as reflection of changing ideas and assumptions. The dialectical development of human ideas is the foundation of the idealist concept of history.

The transformation of a colonial settlement: the Cape Colony 1652–1780

Towards the close of the eighteenth century, the Cape Colony was as unlikely a creation of Dutch enterprise as one could imagine. Although the colony by 1780 contained, all told, far fewer people than the Netherlands, it encompassed an area many times larger than the home country. The only urban settlement of importance was Cape Town. Most of the free colonists of predominantly European descent practised extensive forms of agriculture based upon the employment of slaves and native peoples and devoted to the production of wheat, wine and livestock.[1] These agricultural activities were the foundation of ways of life and outlooks on the world quite different from anything to be found in Europe. Even the small urban population of Cape Town had a distinctive character of its own. A basic historical question about this settlement is 'Why were the predominantly European settlers of this Dutch colony so unlike Europeans in the way they lived?'

The European background

Northwest Europe, from which a majority of officials and free immigrants were drawn, was in the seventeenth century experiencing a period of rapid economic development and population growth.[2] The expansion of trade with other areas of Europe and the outside world was breaking down regional self-sufficiency; the trend was away from subsistence activities and towards market ones. The expansion of trade and industry spurred urban growth. Accompanying these changes and giving them further impetus were political and organizational developments. These developments were particularly marked in the Netherlands, which was dominated by its town-based merchant class.[3] Banks and joint stock companies (of which the Dutch East India Company (*Verenigde Oost-Indische Compagnie*, VOC) was an example) were two important institutions early adopted here which facilitated the investment of capital in trade and industry.

Despite the important developments in trade and industry, agriculture still dominated the European economy. Even in economically advanced countries such as the Netherlands four out of five people lived on and off the land. The way in which agriculture was practised, however, underwent important changes. The rising population and the increasing number of urban dwellers, who no longer fed themselves, stimulated commercial farming. In areas of high population density these commercial developments went hand in hand with more intensive agricultural practices. Feudal obligations in areas in which they still remained were generally replaced by money payments.

In the early seventeenth century the traditional system of plough agriculture based on a three-course field rotation was still in widespread use over much of northwest Europe. The rotation involved a sequence of winter grain, spring grain and fallow.[4] Agriculture was typically carried on in open fields, in which individual farmers cultivated scattered strips of land. The village (the form of settlement associated with this system) tended to control the crops that were cultivated in individual fields. The livestock held by the villagers was pastured on waste and forest land surrounding the arable fields, but were turned loose in the stubble after harvest. This practice helped fertilize the arable lands and was an important element in the agricultural system. In areas where grazing was limited oats were frequently cultivated for the draught animals; in these circumstances horses were preferred to oxen. The village regulated the number of livestock that an individual might pasture on common land.

By the mid-seventeenth century the agricultural system described above was superseded in a few areas of high population density by a new one that made more effective use of the land resources. The new system, the adoption of which is known as the agricultural revolution, had three components: (*a*) the introduction of fodder crops in the rotation system, often after land consolidation; (*b*) the improvement of implement design and the invention of new ones; (*c*) the improvement of livestock quality. The cultivation of new fodder crops was the crucial element in the new system.[5] First, the additional amounts of fodder enabled more livestock to be kept; the livestock, in turn, produced more manure for the fertilization of arable lands. Second, the fodder crops (clover, turnips) improved the fertility of the soils on which they were grown. The net result of the agricultural revolution was to increase crop yields per acre through closer integration of arable and livestock husbandry without the use of chemical fertilizer.

The change-over from the traditional three-field systems to more intensive ones was usually accompanied by widespread changes in rural institutions and the way in which land resources were allocated. The open field was poorly adapted to a system in which individuals were investing large amounts of time on the rearing of livestock. The intensification of agriculture frequently went hand in hand with the enclosure of fields and the consolidation of individual land holdings. The creation of single farm units dealt a heavy blow to village life and weakened the hold of the community on an individual's economic decisions, fostering individualistic or middle class values. But even where older agricultural practices survived, the general trend towards market economies was weakening the power of the village community in relation to the individuals comprising it.

The Low Countries with their high population densities were one of the first areas of Europe to experience the agricultural revolution. In seventeenth-century Holland, there were over a hundred persons per square mile (40 persons per km^2).[6] The commercial and urban developments added further impetus to the adoption of more intensive agricultural practices. The smallness of Holland combined with the well-developed network of canals[7] fostered the developments already under way as a result of population pressure and commercial activity. The intensification of agriculture was accompanied by an increasing labour specialization in rural areas. A variety of village craftsmen found employment in manufacturing equipment and providing services to the farming community.[8]

The factors behind the emergence of the Protestant religions in sixteenth and seventeenth century Europe were numerous and the issues it raises are many and complex. However, the growth of a creed with greater emphasis on individual freedom does not appear to have been unrelated to developments in the economic sphere. The importance Protestant creeds in general and Calvinism in particular placed on such values as thrift, hard work, soberness and the like were well adapted to the needs of Europe's emerging middle class.

The majority of people who freely arrived in South Africa in the seventeenth and early eighteenth centuries whether settler or official, and notwithstanding many differences, shared the common northwest European background described above. The most important elements of this background were a common technical heritage, and individualistic or middle-class values. Whatever an individual's position might have been in this society he would not have been unfamiliar with its main economic and social priorities. This heritage provided an important basis of understanding among all classes of officials and immigrants in South Africa and constituted the starting point from which future relationships in the new land were to develop.

The failure of intensive agriculture, 1652–80

In 1652 the VOC established a settlement at the Cape to provide fresh produce and supplies to its ships trading in Asia. The settlement was conceived of as a supply station rather than a colony.[9] The initial idea was to confine the settlement to a small, easily defensible portion of the Cape Peninsula. This plan in turn rested on two central assumptions. The first assumption was that local Khoikhoi pastoralists would be eager and able to supply the Company with livestock. The second assumption was that the settlement would produce enough grain, fruit and vegetables to support itself and supply visiting ships.

The early experiences of Van Riebeeck, the first commander of the Cape, put these assumptions to the test. It soon became apparent that the Khoikhoi were not eager to trade with the Dutch. Although Van Riebeeck made the most of the first real opportunity he had to trade with the cattle-rich 'Saldanhar' people, the results were meagre. In aggravation Van Riebeeck feasted his eyes on the large herd of Khoikhoi animals. He wrote in the official journal:

The Saldanhars with thousands of cattle and sheep came so close to our fort that their cattle nearly mingled with ours. Could not, however, get the bartering properly under way . . . It is very sad to behold such fine herds of cattle and to be unable to purchase anything worthwhile.[10]

Van Riebeeck would not have hesitated to take what cattle he wanted by force had not his instructions – designed to create an atmosphere of mutual trust between Europeans and Khoikhoi – explicitly forbidden such a course of action.

Today we had ample opportunity of depriving them [the Saldanhars] of 10,000 head of cattle had we been allowed to do so. If we are ordered to do this, it can always be done at some future date; this would suit us even better, for the Saldaniers trust us more as the days go by. Once we had possession of so many cattle, we could maintain an adequate supply by breeding; moreover we should have no fear of the English touching here and spoiling the cattle trade with the natives.[11]

Although trade improved somewhat as the Khoikhoi acquired a taste for European trade goods, and Europeans became more familiar with Khoikhoi ways, the cattle trade did not reach the level the VOC directors had anticipated when the Cape was first settled. The Khoikhoi valued cattle in their own right, and viewed trade in a very different light from the Dutch.

The assumption that the Cape would yield a rich harvest of produce was like the anticipation of a flourishing livestock trade, soon proven wrong. The European settlers had great difficulty raising crops. The soil was difficult to prepare and their tools proved inadequate for the task.[12] Van Riebeeck also found it difficult to get sustained work out of his poorly paid labourers.[13] A lack of draught animals and strong south-east winds further aggravated the situation.[14] As a result of the failure of these early agricultural efforts the small settlement was unable to produce enough grain even for its own needs, and rice, occupying valuable cargo space on Company ships, had to be imported from the East Indies.

The solution to the Cape's problems of food supplies was seen to lie in stimulating wheat production. This goal Van Riebeeck considered could best be achieved by settling free farmers or free burghers on fertile lands to the east of Table Mountain. Shortly after arriving at the Cape, Van Riebeeck had estimated that these lands could support thousands of farmers, an estimate that clearly assumed a European or Asian system of intensive land use.[15] The image of a small mixed farm was to the fore of Van Riebeeck's thinking when he set up a trial farm in this area. Fields of wheat, rice, oats, tobacco, beans and clover were sown. When some months later Van Riebeeck inspected the farm he found:

the haymakers . . . had gathered a large quantity of hay into heaps and were still busy mowing. The clover was especially fine, being knee high and standing very thick. It will be very useful for the horses during the dry season when there is hardly any grazing for them. As in the fatherland, hay will have to be collected annually for the purpose.[16]

The success of this experiment was followed by the creation of free burghers, who were allocated small (27 acre) plots of land.[17] The establishment of free burghers in effect transferred the main burden of agricultural production from Company to private hands. The belief was that individuals working for themselves would work harder and more effectively than they had as Company employees. It was a belief that was based on the legal and social ideas that were beginning to gain widespread support in Europe. Although the free burghers were given a large degree of freedom to manage their affairs, the Company set the prices at which it would purchase their produce.

The free burghers constituted a new force in the Cape, whose interests were not identical with those of the Company. The free burghers were concerned with making a living and they were not too concerned about how they did it. Although Van Riebeeck was right in thinking free burghers would work harder on their own, he failed to realize that in seeking to make a living, they might do it in ways of their own making.

The servants of the Company from whom the first free burghers were chosen had little capital of their own, and opted for their new status on terms that were not as generous as first appeared. The land granted to them was virtually valueless in its unimproved state. A considerable investment of capital and labour was needed to turn a plot of this shrub-covered land into a productive venture. The land had to be cleared of bushes, fields prepared, fences put up, drainage ditches dug and a farm house and its out buildings erected before it could be said that the land constituted a farm.[18]

An acute shortage of labour prompted the Company to supply the Cape settlement with slaves from Asia and Africa. This action was in keeping with contemporary ideas about colonies, and it would have been surprising had slavery not been introduced at the Cape. The adoption of slavery added an important new ingredient to Cape society that was to have a major impact on the social and economic character of the settlement. The early free burghers were each allowed to purchase two or three slaves on credit.[19] These slaves were put to work on the land, but to begin with slaves proved to be unsatisfactory workers. Many deserted and fled inland, others were intractable and their owners returned them to the Company.[20] There was, however, in spite of early problems no suggestion that slaves should be replaced with free labourers.

A low fixed price that was set for wheat combined with a lack of capital and labour difficulties placed the early free burghers in a difficult economic predicament. The production of wheat along the lines Van Riebeeck had anticipated (that is, the intensive cultivation of small areas) required the investment of far more capital and labour than the free burghers possessed. The first objective of the early settlers was a quick return on the borrowed capital – most of it loaned by the Company – they had invested in their farming operations. An immediate income was needed to maintain themselves and their families and wheat production did not offer them any such prospects for immediate gain. The free burghers, therefore, cultivated wheat in a rudimentary fashion on their small freehold farms while they turned elsewhere to make the additional money they needed to survive.[21] Such labour-intensive methods of wheat cultivation as crop rotation, carefully tended fallows, and heavy manuring of fields – necessary activities for sustained high yields – were abandoned. The colonists needed high returns on their capital and labour investments, not high yields per unit area.

In these circumstances, it is not surprising that the free burghers' production of wheat fell well below the quantity Van Riebeeck expected. The other crops that Van Riebeeck had cultivated on his 'model farm' did not receive much attention. Clover and beans were not grown. A little barley and some rye were grown but not in commercial quantities.

In creating the free burghers, Van Riebeeck had intended that they devote themselves to an intensive integrated system of mixed arable and livestock husbandry. The difficulties associated with arable farming, however, led the early free burghers to place a great deal more emphasis on the rearing of livestock, and to separate the livestock and arable sectors of their farming operations. A number of factors made the rearing of livestock particularly attractive to the free burghers: the possibility of acquiring cheap livestock from the Khoikhoi (who were now more prepared to part with their animals), the low demands that livestock rearing made on capital and labour in the Cape environment, the good demand for meat, and payment in cash for meat and live animals.

The ease with which a free burgher could get started in livestock raising was another factor promoting its development. Once a group of animals had been assembled, it did not require much additional investment of capital or labour. There were large areas of open veld on which the animals could be pastured throughout the year for a minimal payment to the VOC. The adoption of the Khoikhoi practice of putting animals in temporary enclosures over-night made the construction of barns and the cultivation of fodder crops unnecessary. The carrying capacity of the Cape veld was often low, particularly in the summer, and the settlers' animals were dispersed over a wide area, but this was not a problem for the small number of freemen and the VOC who used the pasture so long as the number of livestock was small.

The years between the allocation of the first land grants to free burghers in February 1657 and the departure of Van Riebeeck in May 1662 were among the most crucially formative years in the development of the Cape settlement. During these years emerged the main elements of an extensive system of land use that made the further expansion of the settlement virtually inevitable.

Van Riebeeck was correct in believing that the resources of the Cape were capable of supporting 1,000 families. Initially, however, he did not realize that the type of agriculture capable of supporting such a population might not become established at the Cape. The first few years (1652–6) of agricultural experience had not made it easy for him to assess the position of arable farming. The lack of equipment and the problems with the south-easter diverted attention from more fundamental elements of the agricultural system. It was only after his own experience and those of the colonists that Van Riebeeck was in a position to reassess his earlier appraisals of the agricultural potential of the Cape. But even in his final remarks on the Cape's agriculture there is no clear evidence that he really understood why his first plans for the settlement had not been successful.

But it was clear enough to Van Riebeeck that things had not worked out as he had hoped. In spite of the reasonable land grants Van Riebeeck made to the early colonists, they were obviously struggling to make a living. Indeed, conditions were so bad that some of the first free burghers abandoned the Cape leaving their debts behind them; while others moved into non agricultural activities near the fort. These failures had occurred notwithstanding the fact that the Cape farmer's production costs were often substantially lower than those of his European counterpart.

At the Cape, animals were able to forage for themselves in the open veld. Although the summer pasture in the vicinity of the Cape became extremely sparse most stock survived without additional feed. The winter at this latitude was so mild that there was not need of shelters or stall feeding for the animals. Horses, which did require additional feed, were generally replaced by oxen as draught animals. Thus the Cape farmer did not need to grow fodder crops. After 1656 there are no references to fodder crops in the archival records – apart from barley given to the few horses that were retained by many farmers for riding.

The reliance placed on natural pasture resulted in the wide dispersion of stock over the available land, particularly in the summer. The amount of nutrition available to livestock grazing the unimproved Cape veld was much lower per unit area than that available in the meadows of the Low Countries. One visitor expressed surprise that the animals were able to do so well on the poor fare:

It's amazing that there are still such beautiful and strong oxen to be seen, as they have no meadows rich in grass [to graze] but they must seek their food in the open beside the mountains with the sheep.[22]

Large areas of land of this quality were needed to support each unit of stock. Moreover, in this system a limit was placed on the amount of arable land that could be cultivated in any given locality without jeopardizing the pasture needed by the livestock. In the absence of fodder crops, the stock population that could be supported on a given area of pasture land was tied to its minimum seasonal carrying capacity.

The dispersion of livestock affected the way in which the land set aside for arable purposes could be cultivated. Large quantities of manure were wasted as its collection was impracticable. The lack of manure in turn substantially reduced the intensity with which a given area of arable land could be cultivated. In the absence of heavy manuring and fodder crops in the rotation system more reliance had to be placed on fallows to rejuvenate the soil. The longer periods of fallow that were required for arable land to recover its fertility reduced its productivity (measured over a period of years). A farmer using these extensive methods needed a much larger area of land than he would have required in an intensive arable system to produce the same amount of grain.

A fully-fledged extensive system of mixed farming had emerged at the Cape by 1662. In the instructions that Van Riebeeck left for his successor, this development is clearly recognized. The assessment Van Riebeeck made of the potential agricultural value of the settled portion of the Cape Peninsula, when compared with his earlier views, reveals his changed outlook.

And since the pasture within the limits of the Liesbeecq is so scanty that the Company's cattle protected by a strong guard of soldiers are often compelled to graze over and beyond it . . . and as I personally showed you there is no more land within it [the Liesbeecq] suitable to be ploughed, on account of the stones here and there in the ground, so that it cannot in any way serve for the cultivation of wheat, we thus concur with the opinion the Hon. Van Goens expressed in his instructions and keep it as a firm-rule that never can any more grain land be given out there but it must always remain as common grazing or there will be no food for the cattle of the freemen as well as the Company, which often acquires an abundance by barter, so that the animals would die of hunger, many having died annually from that cause.[23]

An area that Van Riebeeck had argued was capable of supporting a thousand or indeed thousands of farmers was now considered fully occupied with approximately fifteen operating farms. Even if it be assumed that Van Riebeeck seriously overestimated the area of arable land that was available (and his mention of the stony ground suggests he might have) he had not made an error of judgement of this magnitude. Rather his earlier assessment had been made in the light of the intensive agricultural system with which he was familiar. He based his final assessment of the area enclosed by the Liesbeecq River on the assumption that the extensive agricultural methods, which had developed during the second half of his administration, would continue in the future.

The years following Van Riebeeck's departure from the Cape in 1662 were ones of stagnation and slow growth. There was a protracted confrontation with the Khoikhoi in the 1670s, which prevented any talk of further expansion. The free burghers continued to farm under difficult conditions. These conditions were reflected in the low standards of rural living and some farm abandonment. In the mid-1660s many of the colonists were described as poor, and there were some cases of extreme poverty.[24] A number of colonists asked that they be taken back into the VOC's service. At the end of his administration Van Riebeeck's successor, Wagenaer, noted that the free burghers, whom he had initially described as a good-for-nothing crew, made slow progress even when they were hard workers.[25] In the early 1670s the settlers continued to abandon their farms; both old hands and newcomers found it hard to make a living from agriculture.[26]

In 1679 the Cape authorities admitted that it was not possible for a free burgher to live on agriculture alone.

We can even say, if all of these agriculturalists had to subsist entirely from arable farming, and could not haul wood, fish and shoot big game inland now and then for the support of their families the majority of them would sink into poverty.[27]

The economic conditions at the Cape encouraged a reversal of the agricultural intensification process that had occurred in Western Europe. In Europe the increasing pressure of people on the land led to rising land values and the closer integration of arable and stock farming. At the Cape a lower man/land ratio enabled the early free burghers to adopt more extensive agricultural methods. The transition to extensive farming took place before adequate amounts of arable or freehold land were available to produce enough cereals for the settlement. Although the free burghers who persevered were for the most part able to make a living for themselves using extensive techniques, many of them were only able to do so by taking advantage of the off-farm opportunities that were available such as wood hauling, hunting and fishing. The major significance of these first twenty-eight years of European colonization lies in the change-over from intensive to extensive agriculture. Such a change would, however, not have been necessary had the directors of the VOC been prepared to invest the capital that was needed to get intensive agriculture firmly established or set wheat prices at the levels that would have encouraged the free burghers themselves to make the necessary investments. Under these circumstances no expansion would have been necessary and a settlement more in line with the initial intentions of the Company's directors might have emerged.

The new system of farming: the Southwestern Cape, 1680–1780

The failure of the early free burghers to produce enough cereals to meet the needs of the settlement and continued dependence on unreliable Khoikhoi for livestock supplies at last prompted the Company to grasp the nettle it had held for a decade or more and expand the area of the colony. In 1679 a new commander, Simon van der Stel, opened new fertile lands for settlement along the Eerste River at Stellenbosch which lay beyond the sand-covered plain connecting the Cape Peninsula with the rest of Africa.[28] A growing number of new and old free burghers took up land in this area, taking advantage of regulations that allowed them to claim substantial quantities of good alluvial land. The average farm size was between 40 and 80 morgen (90 and 180 acres), and large areas of unalienated land were available for grazing.[29]

The open-ended land policy of Simon van der Stel put extensive agriculture on a secure foundation. The colonists now, for the first time, had adequate quantities of good arable land to support extensive cultivation, and easy access to pasture land on their doorsteps. There were excellent prospects for settlers to make a living for themselves, if they could muster the labour, equipment and livestock needed to take advantage of the situation.

The number of settlers grew quickly and so did the production of wheat, wine and livestock. Extensive farming was proving profitable, particularly in years of high prices. As more and more people took out land in the area, the established settlers at Stellenbosch sought to limit further growth. In their eyes, each new farm reduced slightly the amount of grazing and, more significantly, added additional livestock to the unalienated pasture lands. Their complaints did not go unheeded, and in 1687 van der Stel stopped granting freehold land in the Stellenbosch area and showed new settlers to lands in a hitherto unsettled area along the Berg River.[30]

The system of land allocation that was in use in the Stellenbosch area from 1680 to 1687 produced a pattern of landholding not inappropriate to the extensive methods of land use that had evolved at the Cape. The most significant feature of the pattern of landholding was neither the generally large size of the freehold farms nor their riverside locations, but the relatively small proportion of the total land area given over to them. There was, in other words, a high proportion of unallocated VOC (pasture) land compared to freehold (arable) land. At Stellenbosch the ratio was about fifteen to one. The long distances between the farms provoked unfavourable comment from visiting

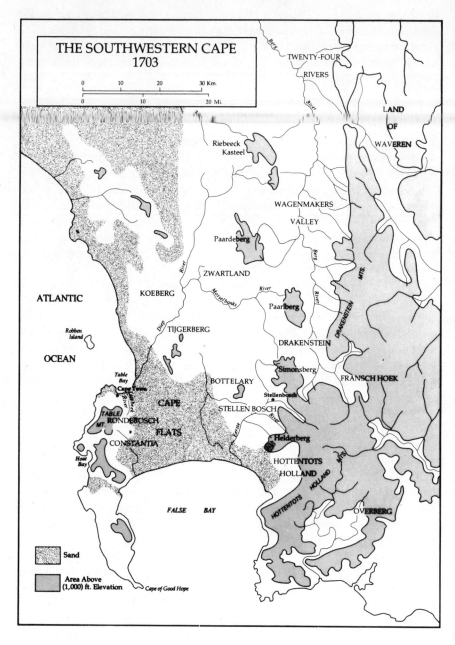

THE SOUTHWESTERN CAPE
1703

0   10   20   30 Km.

0   10   20 Mi.

TWENTY-FOUR
RIVERS

Berg

River

LAND
OF
WAVEREN

Riebeeck
Kasteel

WAGENMAKERS
VALLEY

Paardeberg

ZWARTLAND

ATLANTIC

KOEBERG

Robben
Island

OCEAN

Meiselbanks   River

Berg   River

Paarlberg

River

DRAKENSTEIN MTS.

DRAKENSTEIN

Drag   TIJGERBERG

Simonsberg

FRANSCH HOEK

Table
Bay

Cape Town

River

BOTTELARY

Stellenbosch

TABLE
MT.   RONDEBOSCH

CAPE

STELLEN BOSCH

FLATS

Helderberg

CONSTANTIA

Hout
Bay

Eerste   River

HOTTENTOTS
HOLLAND

HOLLAND MTS.

FALSE   BAY

HOTTENTOTS

OVERBERG

Sand

Area Above
(1,000) ft. Elevation   Cape of Good Hope

commissioner H. A. Van Reede, who criticised the lack of planning in the allocation of land.[31]

Van Reede's criticism, however, was not really justified. Had van der Stel imposed a more rigid system of land allocation based on a regular survey before he had become familiar with the extensive methods of farming at the Cape, he would likely have placed agricultural activities within an inappropriate and confining framework with undesirable economic consequences. Although the 'first come, first served' principle resulted in an irregular pattern of farms of different shapes and sizes, it gave settlers an opportunity to select an economic quantity of good arable land. In a system of land allocation based on geometric principles good arable land would likely have remained in VOC ownership and consequently would have been available to colonists for use as pasture only, while much poor land would probably have been allocated as freehold farms.

The open system of land allocation adopted at Stellenbosch enabled a number of important questions concerning the land requirements of extensive mixed farming to be resolved in the course of the area's development. The amount of land that was needed for a settler to mount a viable farming operation was not specified in advance (in an arbitrary manner) but was left open. Neither was the question as to what the proper proportions between pasture and arable land ought to be decided in the pre-settlement planning stage. Both issues were left to be resolved in the course of the area's development. The system adopted was well suited to the circumstances it was designed to meet. The general lack of knowledge about the Cape's system of extensive farming demanded the adoption of a flexible plan which avoided the specification of potentially unrealistic land-use goals in advance of an area's settlement.

In the three decades after 1687 the area of the colony expanded steadily to accommodate new settlers of many different social, national and economic backgrounds. The general land policy of reserving large areas of land as pasture remained in force. This policy meant that each land owner, taking into account mountain and sandy areas, controlled on average an area of almost 3 square miles, which included a 'small' freehold farm (60 morgen) and the large area of unalienated land surrounding it. The effect of this land system was to scatter the population across the countryside. In 1720 the overall population density of rural areas of the Cape was approximately two people per square mile. This population density is more typical of purely pastoral economies than it is of a mixed economy devoted to arable and livestock husbandry.

Although there emerged at the Cape a pattern of landholding that differed from anything to be found in Holland, it was still an unmistakable reflection of Dutch middle-class thinking. If concessions had been made to the circumstances of the Cape, these concessions did not jeopardize the basic underlying values of Dutch middle-class society. The idea that it was proper for farmers to own and work as much land as their resources permitted was never questioned. The expansion of the colony, in fact, preserved and entrenched the middle-class ideal of private land ownership. Indeed so basic was the concept that the idea of using slaves to make it work appeared quite logical.

The Cape system of landholding might have looked very different if the principle of private land ownership had not been so widely entrenched. Under another principle of organization a system of shifting or open field cultivation based on communal villages might have arisen. This kind of system – sounder from an ecological point of view – would have been associated with its own distinctive social values. However, such a system was out of the question in view of the fundamental assumptions of Dutch officials and settlers.

The adoption of an extensive system of landholding led to the dispersion of the rural population. The scattering of the farmers over a wide area increased the average distances that separated them from each other and from urban centres. Goods and services had to be transported over greater distances than would have been necessary had a more intensive system of agriculture been adopted. In this situation high transportation costs were inevitable. Not only did Cape farmers have to travel longer distances, because of the extremely low population density, but also there were few people among whom the costs of providing the necessary transportation facilities for a given area could be divided.

In view of these conditions, it was logical that the ox-waggon became the most popular vehicle for transporting farm produce. Although oxen are much slower and more cumbersome than horses, they were much better adapted to the heavy hauling necessary to negotiate the rough tracks of the Cape's rural areas. Moreover and unlike horses, oxen were able to feed themselves along the road by foraging in the veld. In the summer months, however, the available pasture was often extremely scanty. Even oxen went hungry and hauled their loads even more slowly than normal.

This form of transportation did little to reduce the isolation of farmers from each other and the urban centres, and worked against the specialized division of labour. It encouraged a farmer to rely heavily on his own resources because of the difficulty and expense involved in hiring a specialist. The extent to which the division of labour was retarded at the Cape is clearly evident from the failure of rural areas to generate villages. The vast area of country beyond the Cape flats was unable to support more than the one tiny village at Stellenbosch.[32] The farmers of Drakenstein were thus obliged to travel from 10 to 30 miles or more to obtain the services of a blacksmith, mason, waggon-maker or of any other artisan. This situation favoured the wealthier farmers who were able to set up specialized services on their estates.

The expansion of the settlement created a demand for more labourers. This demand was largely met by importing more slaves, who were sold to settlers on credit by the Company. More affluent settlers employed white servants in supervisory positions. The less affluent settlers could not afford slaves and for the most part worked their own land employing extra workers when they were needed.[33] The Khoikhoi, whose traditional communities slowly disintegrated under the impact of European settlement, were particularly useful as a source of casual labour for those settlers having no slaves, but also found employment on large estates, especially at harvest time. A Company official, who was stationed at Stellenbosch, has provided a vivid description of the Khoikhoi worker.

The natives on this side of the mountain enthusiastically hire out their labour for a modest wage, and toil more submissively than Spartan helots. They are apt in applying their hands to unfamiliar tasks. Thus they readily acquire the veterinary skills to cure scab in sheep, and they make faithful and efficient herds. They train oxen for use in ploughing; and if put in charge of a wagon, coach or cart, they are found exceedingly quick at inspanning or outspanning or guiding a team. Some of them are very accomplished riders, and have learned to break horses and master them . . . They chop wood, mind the fire, work in the kitchen, prune vines, gather grapes, or work the wine press industriously . . . Their wives and daughters make reliable washer women and busy chars. They wash plates and dishes, clean up dirt, gather sticks from the fields round-about, light the fires, cook well, and provide cheap labour for the Dutch.[34]

In 1713 the Khoikhoi near the Cape were decimated by smallpox, and their importance as a source of labour in the arable area declined sharply.[35]

The Cape administration found it increasingly difficult to control the activities of the colonists who sought opportunities on the wider frontier created by the expansion of the settlement. The illicit livestock trade with Khoikhoi peoples of the interior was lucrative enough to spawn a group of professional frontier traders who acted as middlemen for the Khoikhoi and the farmers of Stellenbosch and Drakenstein.[36] Although colonists were occasionally apprehended while engaged in illicit trading, the frontier was too wide and the number of Company officials too few to stop it. The decrees issued and re-issued against trade with the Khoikhoi are testimony to the inability of the Company to control frontier activity.[37] The situation demanded more effective policing of the frontier rather than the promulgation decrees with heavy sentences for the contravention of laws every trader was confident he could avoid.

As the number of animals comprising their flocks and herds increased the colonists did not hesitate to use the pasture lands beyond the settled areas. In the dry summer months it became common for farmers to send their livestock inland under the care of a son or trusted slave. This incipient system of transhumance received a setback when Simon van der Stel, anxious to reassert Company control of the frontier, ordered free burghers to keep their livestock within a day's journey of their freehold properties.[38]

In 1703, however, a new administration under the former Governor's son reversed this policy and began issuing grazing permits at no charge to those who applied for them. The holder of an early grazing permit was entitled to the exclusive use of a designated area for a period of three to four months. The standard period of a permit's validity was soon extended to six months, and general criteria were gradually established to define its limits. The basic rule was that no grazing permit would be issued to a new applicant within an hour's walking distance of the centre of an existing one.[39] In practice this meant that each permit holder had exclusive control of a minimum of 6,000 acres (2,420 ha).[40] In 1714 a small fee was charged for a grazing permit or loan farm as such a permit came to be known.[41] In the same year permission to cultivate wheat, which up to that time had been granted on an individual basis, was made a standard concession. The changing regulations affecting the use of grazing permits or loan farms enabled many colonists who could not afford a freehold farm to establish themselves as independent farmers on the frontier.

The frontier, in addition to trade and pasture, offered incomparable hunting opportunities of which colonists had availed themselves from the earliest times. Small hunting parties were constantly setting out in search of game, particularly hippopotamus and eland. Such expeditions might last a week or more. A few colonists made careers for themselves as professional elephant hunters, and penetrated deep into country.[42]

In 1717 the VOC decided not to encourage further European migration to the Cape and to continue to rely on slave labour for the future development of the colony.[43] Cape authorities were ordered to stop giving out land in freehold to arable farmers, as a surplus of arable produce was now a detriment of the Company. This decision, however, was not as important for settlement as it might otherwise have been, because land was still available on loan. Many arable farmers had in earlier times commenced farming on a loan farm, a portion of which was later converted into a freehold farm. After 1717 an individual could acquire land for his own use through inheritance, by purchase, or by leasing a loan farm. In practice there was little distinction between freehold land and loan farms, whose leases became so secure that the fixed improvements (which could be sold) came to reflect the value of the whole property.[44]

The weak demand for Cape wine and wheat made things difficult for arable farmers. The effects of the slack market, however, were not felt evenly by all farmers, but varied according to the size of their operations. In general large estates were more efficient than small ones, whose production costs tended to increase with time. The lack of a reliable and inexpensive group of artisans to serve them was one barrier to efficient production keenly felt by small and medium producers. Baron Van Imhoff, who inspected the Cape in 1743, remarked:

It seems incredible that a mason and a carpenter each earns from eight to nine schellingen a day and in addition receives food and drink and withal does not do as much as a half trained artisan in Europe. It is a burden this colony cannot bear and it certainly has a prejudicial effect on agriculture.[45]

This situation was largely a consequence of the dispersed pattern of settlement, which worked against the division of labour. The larger producers could avoid the costs of hiring independent artisans by establishing their own specialized estate workshops, which were manned by skilled slaves.[46]

The small producer was also hit hard by the catastrophic decline in the number of Khoikhoi workers. Expensive slave help had to be hired from other colonists, at busy times in the agricultural year, because marginal farmers could not afford more than a few costly slaves of their own.[47] More affluent farmers, although they too were affected by increased dependence on slave labour, were able to take advantage of size to achieve some economies of scale. In a large operation such economies could be achieved by dividing farm tasks among a dozen or so slaves, each of whom might have a special skill.

The ability of a young person to take up arable farming was largely determined by the amount of capital he or she was able to command. A number of sources of capital, both public and private, were available to Cape farmers in the eighteenth century, but by far the most important was inheritance (actual or potential). Under the Cape system of partible inheritance, an estate of a free burgher was normally divided equally between the children and surviving spouse.[48] Each child, regardless of sex, was entitled to an equal portion of the children's half of the estate. Inheritance portions could be altered if a will were made, but no spouse or child could be disinherited of more than one-half of his or her standard portion.

The operation of the demand and supply factors of arable farming was reflected in a general tendency for the size of arable operations to increase. This tendency is clearly reflected in the increasing number and the changing distribution of slaves employed by arable farmers. The number of male slaves in arable farming increased from 1,500 in 1716 to 2,800 in 1770; the number of farmers who owned one or two slaves declined, but an increasing number of farmers owned ten or more.[49] Additional evidence of trends in arable farming is to be found in the records of deceased estates, which reveal that many small farmers were up to their ears in debt and left no assets at all.[50] As small producers were eliminated other individuals became exceptionally wealthy. In the period 1771–80 several colonists left estates worth over 30,000 guilders; the largest was valued at 225,000 guilders.[51]

Frontier expansion, 1703–80

As the opportunities in arable farming declined, more and more colonists became stock farmers and took out loan farms at ever-increasing distances from Cape Town.[52] In a little more than sixty years stock farmers or *trekboers* increased the area of South Africa occupied by people of European descent almost ten-fold. The stock farmers increased at a rapid rate while the number of arable farmers remained all but static. By 1780 over two-thirds of the independent farmers at the Cape were engaged in stock farming.

The rapid expansion in the eighteenth century of the area of South Africa permanently occupied by European settlers was not part of a deliberate policy of colonization. Each individual who moved into the African interior to become a stock farmer on a loan farm made this decision himself without encouragement or direction from the VOC. In fact, measures were adopted from time to time with a view to slowing down and even stopping the rapid dispersal of settlers away from Cape Town. The expansion of the Colony that occurred in this period is thus sharply differentiated from the earlier expansion of arable farming which took place under the direction and supervision of Van Riebeeck and the van der Stels. Yet, if frontier expansion was not encouraged it did take place within a legal framework set up and administered by the VOC; although Company control was often weak and ineffective, particularly as it applied to the treatment of native peoples, it was never entirely absent. It permitted the occupation of new areas to take place in a reasonably orderly fashion.

The rapidity with which much of South Africa was settled by European colonists suggest that the frontier was perceived as an area of opportunity, in spite of its isolation and dangers. Moreover, the attractiveness of the frontier seems to have been unrelated to its immediate or even long-term commercial potential. The *trekboers* put hundreds of miles of open veld between themselves and their only market at Cape Town. This rapid movement of settlers into the interior was not anticipated by the VOC and its meaning remains a vital question for modern scholars of European expansion and frontier settlement.

The first question that needs to be answered is, 'What attracted people to the frontier?' This question can, perhaps, be rephrased as, 'What was it that people saw in the frontier that made them want to settle on it?' There is no question that people moved onto the frontier in considerable numbers. Why? This question must be answered by showing that, for a considerable number of people, it was a reasonable course of action.

A satisfactory explanation of frontier expansion must be able to show that the frontier offered certain people, in specific economic and social circumstances, positive advantages over the other alternatives that might have presented themselves. The availability of 'free' land by itself, is not necessarily correctly considered a positive advantage. In the first place, frontier land was not free; it had to be taken from native peoples. In the second place, free land is worthless unless it is capable of being effectively used. The real question of frontier settlement to be answered, therefore, concerns the kind of living it offered European settlers and the advantages that living had over the available, or, more precisely, the perceived alternatives.

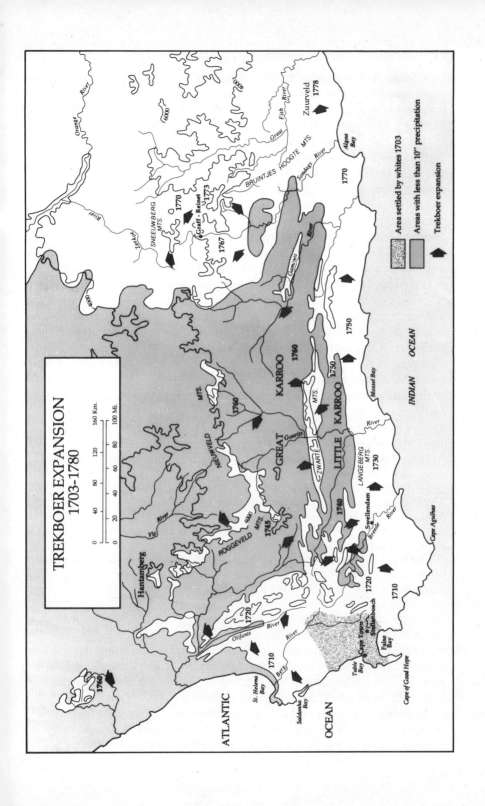

TREKBOER EXPANSION
1703-1780

0   20   40   60   80   100 Mi.

0 40 80 120 160 Km.

Area settled by whites 1703

Areas with less than 10" precipitation

Trekboer expansion

ATLANTIC

OCEAN

St. Helena Bay

Saldanha Bay

1710

Olifants River

1720

Berg River

1720

Table Bay

Cape Town

Stellenbosch

False Bay

Cape of Good Hope

1710

1720

Breede River

Swellendam

1740

LANGEBERG MTS.

1730

Cape Agulhas

Mossel Bay

River

LITTLE KARROO

1750

ZWARTE MTS.

Gouritz River

GREAT KARROO

1750

1760

1760

INDIAN OCEAN

1770

Algoa Bay

Zuurveld

1778

Fish River

Great

Sundags River

BRUINTJES HOOGTE MTS.

Gamtoos River

1773

Graff - Reinet

1770

1767

SNEEUWBERG MTS.

6000

Orange River

River

River

Zeekoe

4000

6000

Hantamberg

1720

NIEUWVELD MTS.

Vis River

1745

ROGGEVELD MTS.

4000

1760

1760

In South Africa, frontier settlement was characterized by a large degree of subsistence economic activity. Indeed, had it not been possible for settlers to support themselves in large measure from such activities, it is unlikely that frontier expansion could have occurred as rapidly as it did. Although practically all scholars acknowledge the importance of subsistence activity, particularly in the early years of settlement, the interesting question is whether this activity was an early phase in the commercial development of an area or a phenomenon in its own right. In South Africa where a commercial economy developed slowly, it is possible to examine this question in a setting free of the complications that are associated with rapid commercial developments, which occurred in much of North America. If it could be shown that, even in remote and isolated areas, commercial considerations were paramount, any need of a separate explanation of frontier settlement would have been eliminated.

One school of thought has maintained that, even in areas largely isolated from outside markets, commercial considerations were never far from the settlers' minds. In support of this position it has been pointed out, notably by Neumark, that however remote the frontier, settlers always maintained some commercial ties with the outside world.[53] The crucial issue here is not the existence of commercial ties themselves, but rather whether such ties were profitable from a commercial point of view. If the commercial ties were not profitable, they can scarcely be said to have provided a commercial motive for settlement. What evidence there is suggests that the trade maintained by settlers of the frontier with the outside world was, from a commercial point of view, unprofitable.

John Barrow, an English observer of late eighteenth-century South Africa, made the following observation.

The distance [separating the frontier from Cape Town] is a serious inconvenience to the farmer. . . . If he can contrive to get together a wagon load or two of butter or soap, to carry with him to Cape Town once a year, or once in two years, in exchange for clothing, brandy, coffee, a little tea and sugar and a few other luxuries, which his own district has not yet produced, he is perfectly satisfied. The consideration of profit is out of the question. A man who goes to Cape Town with a single wagon from the Sneuwberg must consume, as least, sixty days out and home.[54]

This explanation could be rephrased: a frontier farmer would not be acting rationally were he to contemplate a 120 day return trip to Cape Town with the expectation of making a profit. The frontier farmers (all of whom were able to appreciate what the distance separating them from Cape Town meant) did not think in terms of profit and were, therefore, satisfied if such a trip paid for certain luxuries which they particularly desired.

Additional evidence against the commercial interpretation of frontier settlement in isolated areas of poor communications is provided by an examination of the rates of settlement, and comparing them with the market for frontier produce. Frontier settlement proceeded regardless of the fluctuations in the market for the produce of the frontier. For example, new settlement continued at rates that showed no correlation with the fluctuations in the prices that meat was fetching in the market at Cape Town. In the early 1740s the market was particularly depressed, yet the settlement of new frontier areas showed no evidence of decline.[55]

The nature of frontier expansion becomes more rather than less puzzling if commercialism is rejected as the major factor behind much frontier settlement. Why were European colonists eager to take up and settle land without immediate commercial value, often in defiance of government decrees and without government protection? In terms of conventional economic theory a subsistence economy represents a step backwards from a commercial one, because the subsistence producer sacrifices the advantages that arise from specialization based upon a division of labour. On the acceptance of this theory the frontier would not have been a desirable place to settle.

It is conceivable that the frontier was settled in the hope of commercial farming by settlers who only discovered that such farming was impracticable after they had moved. In North America the assumption that farming would with time become profitable was not altogether unfounded and might indeed have been a factor in the settlement of many of the more accessible areas. However, such an explanation seems unlikely to apply to frontier settlers in South Africa. These settlers were almost certainly aware that the distances from markets at which they took up their new homes were such that farming was and would be at a near subsistence level for decades. And yet, settlers moved into the interior in large numbers.

One possible explanation of frontier settlement is that the frontier was attractive, because it offered settlers individual liberty. This explanation rests on substantiating two points. First, one would need to establish that the idea of individual freedom was a strong element of the cultural heritage of the *trekboers*. Second, that this element was strong enough to persuade many individuals to take decisions which were, from an economic point of view, irrational. Although the desire for individual freedom was very likely a factor in encouraging the movement of people onto the frontier, whether or not it was a critical factor would need to be established by appropriate empirical evidence. We would have to be able to show that the prestige of an independent livelihood, even when associated with isolation and poverty, was such that frontier life was preferred by many, especially those near the bottom of society, to a more secure, but dependent existence in settled regions.

The topic of individual freedom and its relationship to land would warrant far more detailed attention than I can give it here. Nevertheless, progress towards an understanding of frontier settlement is possible along another line. The widespread notion that economics and profit are synonymous has led scholars to overlook an aspect of frontier expansion that could be crucial for an understanding of this phenomenon. Boserup and others have shown that in situations where there are low man/land ratios and abundant resources it is possible for a sparse population to make a comfortable living from subsistence or near subsistence activity without hard work.[56] This evidence immediately adds a new dimension to the phenomenon of frontier settlement. If it can be assumed that people in the settled areas on or near the frontier zone were aware of the economic possibilities of frontier life, such awareness would likely have been a major consideration in the decisions that many people made to settle the frontier. It would go a long way to explain why so many people moved into areas that were isolated from supplies and markets.

The evidence presented by Boserup is not in itself an explanation of frontier expansion. It does, however, suggest that frontier living might have been a lot easier than modern scholars have appreciated, and, that, in imposing modern concepts of economics on the frontier situation many scholars might well have underestimated and misinterpreted crucial historical evidence relating to the economic life of the frontier. The ideas and evidence presented by Boserup come as a surprise to us, because almost all modern scholars have assimilated certain economic propositions. One basic economic 'truth' is that the division of labour is the foundation of economic efficiency. This rule translates into the corollary that exchange economies are more efficient than subsistence economies. When a consistent and logical thinker like Neumark confronted the evidence of frontier expansion, he was obliged to adopt one of the following propositions:

(1) The economic law or generalization that exchange economies are more efficient than subsistence ones is false.
(2) The people who freely disassociated themselves from participation in an exchange economy to settle the frontier were economically irrational.
(3) The linkages between frontier settlers and the main economy were a vital part of frontier expansion.

Neumark opted for proposition (3), which led him to exaggerate the commercial (profit-making) relations between the frontier and the outside world, and to ignore the considerable amount of evidence suggesting that many frontier farms were not profitable in the commercial sense. As an economic historian Neumark was loath to adopt proposition (2). In fact, his work was aimed at refuting it. The one solution that Neumark might have adopted to extricate himself from the dilemma he faced he did not evidently consider. This solution would have involved accepting proposition (1). Neumark had no reason to do this since it questioned an assumption that was simply taken for granted.

The interpretation Neumark put forward to account for frontier settlement in South Africa brings to light a major problem that is associated with any theoretical approach (implicit or explicit) to historical understanding. If, on the one hand, one accepts a theory or relationship as true, historical investigation becomes nothing more than a pseudo-empirical verification of its truth. This was the critical weakness of environmental determinism and also of Neumark's work on the frontier. If, on the other hand, one's investigation is concerned with testing a theory to find out whether or not it is supported by empirical evidence it ceases to be historical. It is not, for example, the historian's task to ascertain whether generalizations such as 'exchange economies are more efficient than subsistence ones' is true or not, but that of the economist. The problem of history becoming a discipline in which theories of dubious validity are illustrated, or in which theories of the systematic sciences are tested, is avoided by rejecting the idea that historians are concerned with theories of human behaviour that are imposed upon reality by the researchers themselves.

It might be here objected that my interpretation of frontier settlement replaces Adam Smith with Ester Boserup. In citing Boserup I have been more concerned with her empirical evidence than I have with any general theory. The empirical evidence she cites is important precisely because it shakes our belief in the truth of classical economics. This 'truth' was getting in the way of our interpretations of the evidence. Such an investigation should be conducted outside of any formal theoretical structure which might lead one to misinterpret empirical evidence.

In the above analysis of the frontier I have at best hinted at the reasons why settlers moved onto the frontier. A fuller explanation would demand that the frontier option be assessed in terms of the attractiveness it might have had for a variety of groups in relation to other options that might have existed for these same groups. Only when the frontier movement is understood in the context of what made rational sense to those involved would it be possible to claim that an adequate explanation along idealist lines had been provided. Although my interpretation is still incomplete, the idealist analysis has shown that many frontier settlers could not have anticipated commercial profits from their frontier farming operations.

Resource development in the interior was a reflection of European thought. The previous occupants of the country, the Khoikhoi, had organized themselves along entirely different lines.[57] They recognized a man's right to own stock but not to own pasture. Grazing lands were held in common and the resources of the area were exploited on a nomadic basis. Each group, in theory, remained within an agreed territory which was the 'property' of the whole group. From an ecological point of view, this system was sound – in fact close to the optimum arrangement for sustaining large numbers of stock over prolonged periods of time. There was nothing in the nature of the resources themselves, therefore, that necessitated a settlement pattern of dispersed homesteads. This arrangement was only possible when underlying values stressed the importance of individual rights to land.

The economic life on the frontier that developed within a system of individual landholding provides the key to understanding its social life. The principle of individual grazing rights to land combined with the nature of much of the South African interior led to the dispersal of the stock farmers over an enormous area of land. Each individual farmer was even more isolated from his neighbours than were the arable farmers. On the frontier, the nearest neighbour was normally five to ten miles away. The extremely low population density of this kind of dispersed settlement precluded the growth of villages or of a non farm class of rural dwellers.[48] Every farmer had to be largely independent in meeting his everyday needs. The stock farmer was in no position to copy the arable farmer who managed to overcome some of his isolation problems by internalizing his operation because his resource was unimproved pasture. There was simply no incentive to invest in such a resource-base so long as transportation costs prevented him from reaping much reward from such an investment. The improvement of transportation facilities necessary to encourage capital investment would have placed an intolerable financial burden on each of the frontier regions' few inhabitants.

The lack of services, paradoxically, made frontier inhabitants, if anything, less rather than more hard-working. The general isolation worked against those who attempted improvements and favoured those who sought a living directly from the available resources. The marginal gains to be had from hard toil, of a commercial kind, and the ease of making a livelihood gave frontiersmen considerable amounts of leisure time. In South Africa travellers were apt to describe the *trekboers* as lazy. The Swedish visitor Sparrman described the life of a recently settled frontier district.

All the colonists who follow the grazing business, and particularly those at *Agter Bruintjes-hoogte*, lead an easy and pleasant life. One of these boors usually gets to his plough eight or ten of his fat, or rather pampered oxen; and it is hardly to be conceived, with what little trouble he gets into order a field of moderate size ... So that, always sure of rich harvest from a soil not yet worn out, which is ever responsive to the culture bestowed upon it, he may be almost said merely to amuse himself with the cultivation of it for the bread he wants for himself and his family; while many other husbandmen must sweat and toil themselves almost to death, both for what they use themselves, and for that which is consumed by others.[59]

The lack of outlets on the frontier for investment outside stock farming led to a remarkable uniformity of agricultural operations. If the frontier provided an easy place for a poor man to establish an independent farm, it was a difficult place for anyone to become wealthy. The stock farmer was caught in a vicious circle – transportation improvements required an increase in population density which required better transportation facilities – that kept him at a near subsistence level. Apart from the occasional journey he might make to the Cape to take his produce to market or to collect supplies, the typical stock farmer had few off-farm connections. For decades on end the frontier farmer remained largely cut off from the faster tempo of commercial life of the areas closer to Cape Town.

An implication of the near-subsistence economy of the frontier was the relatively even distribution of wealth among its European inhabitants. A wealthy farmer was worth, perhaps, four or five times as much as a poor one. Although there were some extremely poor *bijwooners* or tenant farmers, they were often younger people who were getting together the capital they needed to start stock farming on their own. A minority of the *bijwooners*, however, never became independent farmers. But even if all Europeans are taken into account, frontier wealth was spread remarkably evenly. The equality of economic worth was further emphasized by the similarity of life styles. The richer *trekboers* were distinguished from others simply by their greater number of stock. In their dress, housing and ways of life there was little to distinguish rich men from poor.

The egalitarian and independent attitudes found on the frontier were fostered by the economic independence of its inhabitants and the even distribution of wealth among them. On his isolated farm each *trekboer* produced practically everything he needed; what he himself could not produce was acquired directly from Cape Town. In other words, each farmer was largely independent of his neighbours for his economic well being. In the extreme conditions of near-subsistence farming found on the South African frontier, a farmer could ignore his neighbours without incurring any economic penalty. If neighbouring *trekboers* quarrelled there was little economic incentive to patch things up as neither of them needed the other's cooperation to maintain his economic position. In this situation of extreme economic independence the spirit of egalitarianism degenerated into one of general quarrelsomeness, and neighbours were often not on speaking terms.[60]

The emergence of an 'intolerant' individualistic society was fostered by the absence of a nonfarm rural population dependent on the farming community. Artisans (wagonmakers, masons, coopers, tailors and the like), retailers, and innkeepers did not exist. Because they are dependent for their economic survival on the goodwill of the entire farming community, people in such occupations tend to be tolerant and flexible in their attitudes and actively promote these values within the whole society. The division of labour, therefore, creates a situation of mutual interdependence among an increasing number of people and makes intolerance and extreme individuality a luxury few can afford. The frontier society of South Africa lacked the glue that a nonfarm rural population provided and became, in consequence, excessively atomized.

Yet the frontiersman set some limits to independent behaviour. He was noted for his hospitality. Yet the hospitality the frontier inhabitants accorded strangers was not, as has often been claimed, primarily a reaction to the loneliness of their isolated existence. The man who would welcome strangers would not infrequently go months on end without speaking to his neighbours. If the desire for social contact with other Europeans had been great, close neighbours would more readily have patched up their quarrels for the sake of enjoying each other's company. There is, however, a good economic reason why the frontier boer should have been so hospitable to travellers. In a country without any inns, guest houses or stores, the traveller was entirely dependent on the farmers living along his route for refreshments and supplies. Sooner or later all frontier farmers had to make journeys to and from the Cape, and they all benefited from this informal system of reciprocity. Another area in which the frontiersmen cooperated with each other was in the defense of their property against 'Bushmen' or San; the very existence of the white frontier community depended on it.

The fact that frontier society was based on slave and Khoikhoi servants added an important dimension not found in many other colonial frontier societies. The *trekboer* treated his slaves and servants with extreme cruelty, and there was precious little they could do about it. There were few alternatives available for the Khoikhoi whose lands and stock had been taken but to work for a *trekboer*. Once on a *trekboer*'s loan farm, the law offered the Khoikhoi individual little protection. In any event, on his isolated farm a *trekboer* was virtually a law unto himself. In these circumstances there was nothing constraining an individual *trekboer* from meting out excessive punishment to those he despised as heathens.

The Calvinism that the *trekboer* took with him onto the frontier was peculiarly well suited to the environment in which he found himself. 'By virtue of his religion, he justified his right to dominate the heathen by whom he was surrounded. They fell outside the pale, and their claims, therefore, could never compete on equal terms with those of the Christian group'.[61] It reinforced and rationalized the frontier way of life, but it seems unlikely that the *trekboer*'s religion was mainly responsible for his value system. Frontier economic conditions (as they developed within the VOC's legal framework) in themselves appear to offer an adequate explanation for the rise of extreme individualism, and the poor treatment meted out to servants and slaves.

Summary and conclusion

The crucial factors in the evolution of a new society in South Africa can now be summarized. First, there was the colonial-modified, European background of the settlement. This background provided the colony with its basic institutions including general principles of land tenure and inheritance and the acceptance of slavery. The important contribution to the new society was made by Europeans, not so much as individuals, but as vehicles through which European institutions and modes of thought were transplanted to a new setting. It was the setting up of a distinctive European framework of government and landholding, which European settlers understood, in the African setting that laid the foundation for a new society. Second, there was a sparse population with its low man/land ratio. An economic consequence of this ratio was to reduce the value of land in relation to that of capital and labour. Or briefly, while land was scarce and labour plentiful in Europe, the reverse applied to the Cape. Third, there was the general dependence of Cape farmers on passing ships for a market for most of their produce. This isolation from the world's markets was mainly responsible for the general economic depression which hung over the area for the greater part of the eighteenth century.

These three factors interacted with each other to produce the main features of a new African society of European origin. The institutions coupled with an abundance of land were primarily responsible for the emergence of an extensive and individualistic system of agriculture based on slave and native labour. The low prices of arable produce in the eighteenth century hastened the dispersion of *trekboers*. Had a better market existed for wine and wheat the subdivision of farms might have made economic sense, and instead of dispersion a process of intensified land use might well have been set in motion. In the actual market circumstance, a commitment to the private holding and control of land fostered the emergence of a frontier society based on extensive individualistic stock farming, in which European origins became difficult to discern, but were everywhere present.

Postscript

The distinctive forms of Cape life must be understood as historical creations. These creations were not made to a preconceived blueprint but developed logically step by step. The logic of these steps must be established by empirical research and understood as a *process* of thought. For example, Van Riebeeck established free burghers as a logical solution to a problem defined by and solved within a specific framework of thought. The free burghers, the outcome of Van Riebeeck's decision, made their own logical decisions to survive. The decisions, in turn created a new unexpected situation which required new decisions. The historical approach exists because any action is the product of a partial understanding. Nothing ever works out precisely as intended without any side effects or unintended consequences. The historian's task is to make sense of the unpredictable (but logical) way in which human societies have developed. This task is only possible where the sequence of thought expressed in actions can be reconstructed and understood.

References and notes

1 In 1780 the Cape Colony comprised about 10,000 free colonists of European extraction (Dutch, German and Huguenot). There were about 11,000 slaves

(mainly from Asia, Madagascar and Africa). Males greatly outnumbered females in the slave population. There was a small 'free black' population who lived in Cape Town. The number of native Khoikhoi and San is impossible to estimate, but it seems likely at least 10,000 had, by 1780, become clients of white farmers.

2 C. T. Smith, *An historical geography of Western Europe* (London, Longmans, Green, 1967), pp. 428–61.
3 *Ibid.*, p. 458.
4 G. E. Fussell, 'The Agricultural Revolution, 1600–1850', in M. Kranzberg and C. W. Pursell, jr. (eds.), *Technology in Western civilization* (New York, Oxford University Press, 1967), p. 129.
5 B. H. Slicher van Bath, *The agrarian history of Western Europe, A.D. 500–1850* (London, Edward Arnold, 1963), pp. 278–80.
6 G. N. Clark, *The seventeenth century*, 2nd edn. (Oxford, The Clarendon Press, 1947), p. 8.
7 P. Zumthor, *Daily life in Rembrandt's Holland* (London, Weidenfeld and Nicolson, 1962), p. 30.
8 *Ibid.*, p. 27.
9 H. C. V. Leibbrandt, *Précis of the archives of the Cape of Good Hope: letters and documents received, 1649–62* (Cape Town, W. A. Richards and Sons, 1896–99) vol. 1, pp. 1–17.
10 H. B. Thom (ed.), *Journal of Jan van Riebeeck, 1651–62* (Cape Town and Amsterdam, A. A. Balkema, 1954), vol. 1, p. 21.
11 *Ibid.*
12 A. J. du Plessis, 'Die geskiedenis van die graankultuur in Suid-Afrika, 1652–1752', *Annals of the University of Stellenbosch*, **11** (1933), 2–5.
13 *Ibid.*, 4.
14 *Ibid.*, 5.
15 *Journal of Van Riebeeck*, vol. 1, pp. 35–6.
16 *Ibid.*, vol. 2, p. 69.
17 *Ibid.*, vol. 2, p. 88.
18 SAA (South African Archives), C 493, Uitgaande Brieven, pp. 986–7.
19 I. D. MacCrone, *Race attitudes in South Africa* (London, Oxford University Press, 1937), p. 31.
20 *Ibid.*, pp. 32–3.
21 K. M. Jeffreys and S. D. Naudé (eds.), *Kaapse Plakkaatboek, 1652–1795* (Cape Town, Government Printer, 1944–49), vol. 1, pp. 61–2.
22 A. J. Böeseken (ed.) *Belangrike Kaapse documente: memoriën en instructiën, 1657–99* (Cape Town, Government Printer, 1966), p. 186.
23 *Ibid.*, p. 39.
24 SAA, C586, Dagregister, p. 406.
25 *Memoriën en instructiën*, p. 74.
26 SAA, C498, Uitgaande Brieven, p. 972.
27 SAA, C499, Uitgaande Brieven, p. 119.
28 *Ibid.*, p. 514.
29 Deeds Office (Cape Town), Old Stellenbosch Freeholds, vol. 1.
30 SAA, C592, Dagregister, p. 521.
31 H. A. van Reede, 'Journal van zijn verblijf aan de Kaap', *Bijdragen en Mededeellingen van het Historisch Genootschap* (Utrecht), **62** (1941), 122–3.

32 L. Guelke, 'Frontier settlement in early Dutch South Africa', *Annals of the Association of American Geographers,* **66** (1976), 36–7.

33 In 1716, 1,500 slaves were distributed among 226 colonists. Of these, 130 farmers held five or fewer slaves, and 43 farmers held more than ten; KA (Koloniaal Archief, The Hague), Brieven en Papieren van de Caab Overgekomen, No. 4053, Opgaaf-Rollen (1716).

34 G. G. Grevenbroek, 'An elegant and accurate account of the African race living round the Cape of Good Hope commonly called Hottentots' in I. Schapera, (ed.), *The early Cape Hottentots* (Cape Town, The Van Riebeeck Society, 1933), pp. 271–73. On the Khoikhoi as workers, see also L. Fouché and A. J. Böeseken, (eds.) *The diary of Adam Tas, 1705–1706* (Cape Town, Van Riebeeck Society, 1970), pp. 117 and 123; and P. Kolben, *The present state of the Cape of Good Hope* (London, W. Innys, 1731), p. 47.

35 According to one party of Khoikhoi who presented themselves at Cape Town to have new leaders confirmed in office, not one in ten of their people had survived the catastrophe; KA, Brieven en Papieren van de Caab Overgekomen No. 4050, p. 274 (13 February 1714).

36 *Kaapse Plakkaatboek,* vol. 1, p. 262.

37 *Ibid.,* p. 283.

38 *Ibid.,* p. 263.

39 The precise point at which this rule was introduced is not certain, but reference to the use of a watch in pacing out distances in the field occurs as early as 1714.

40 Although in theory, the *leeningsplaats* or loan farm was circular, this theory meant little to the *trekboer* of the eighteenth century. So long as he did not infringe on his neighbours a *trekboer* had de-facto control of all the land he could use, often twice or four times the theoretical minimum.

41 A. J. Böeseken (ed.), *Resolusies van die politieke raad* (Cape Town, Government Printer, 1957–62), vol. 4, p. 412.

42 A good account of hunting expeditions at the Cape is O. F. Mentzel, *A geographical–topographical description of the Cape of Good Hope* (Cape Town, van Riebeeck Society, 1921–1944), vol. 3, pp. 125–6. Mentzel lived at the Cape in the early part of the eighteenth century.

43 SAA, C436, Inkomende Brieven, p. 604. The views of the members of the Cape Political Council, whose advice was sought before the decision on slavery was announced, are in *Reports of Chavonnes and his Council and of van Imhoff, on the Cape* (Cape Town, Van Riebeeck Society, 1918). All but one councillor argued in favour of the retention of slavery.

44 This statement is based on an examination of the prices paid at public auctions for the fixed improvements of the loan farms.

45 *Reports of Chavonnes,* p. 137.

46 Items of equipment are listed under workshop headings in inventories of the larger estates; SAA, Weeskamer (Orphan Chamber), M.O.O.C. Series 8: Inventarissen, vols. 1–17.

47 Guelke, 'Frontier Settlement', 33.

48 G. M. Theal, *History of South Africa before 1795,* 4th edn., (London, George Allen and Unwin, 1927), vol. 3, p. 360.

49 Data were based on KA, Brieven en Papieren van de Caab Overgekomen, Nos. 4144 and 4240 (Opgaaf-Rollen) (1716 and 1770).

50 In the period 1731–1742 the average debt of all estates with a gross value of less than 10,000 guilders was 4,170 guilders, a whopping 78.6 per cent of the average gross assets; data from SAA Weeskamer (Orphan Chamber), M. O. O. C. Series 8, Inventarissen, vols. 5–8.

51 SAA, St 18/31: Inventarissen, No. 17 (24–26 June 1776).

52 Independent stock farmers comprised one tenth of 260 agriculturalists in 1716. Their numbers increased to 225 in 1746 and 600 in 1770, at which time they made up over two-thirds of all independent Cape farmers. KA, Brieven en papieren van de Kaap overgekomen, Nos. 4053, 4144 and 4240 (Opgaaf–Rollen).

53 S. D. Neumark, *Economic influences on the South African frontier* (Stanford, Stanford University Press, 1957), pp. 5, 17 and 39.

54 J. Barrow, *An account of travels into the interior of Southern Africa* (London, T. Cadwell, jr. and W. Davies, 1801) vol. 2, p. 331.

55 Guelke, 'Frontier settlement', 40–1.

56 E. Boserup, *The conditions of agricultural growth* (London, George Allen and Unwin, 1965), pp. 43–55.

57 R. Elphick, *Kraal and castle: Khoikhoi and the founding of white South Africa* (New Haven, Yale University Press, 1977), pp. 57–62.

58 Guelke, 'Frontier settlement', 36–7.

59 A. Sparrman, *A voyage to the Cape of Good Hope, 1771–76* (Cape Town, Van Riebeeck Society, 1977) vol. 2, pp. 130–1.

60 H. Lichtenstein, *Travels in Southern Africa in the years 1803, 1804, 1805 and 1806*, translated by A. Plumptre (Cape Town, Van Riebeeck Society, 1928–9), vol. 1, p. 116.

61 MacCrone, *Race attitudes*, pp. 127–9.

6

A concluding comment

The idealist philosophy provides a foundation for the development of an empirical approach to human and regional geography in keeping with the traditional objectives of human geography. Although the philosophy of idealism is not concerned with defining the discipline of geography or historical geography, the way in which the discipline is defined has in fact been greatly shaped by philosophical ideas. In advocating idealism as a philosophy it is not my intention to create yet another 'new' geography. In fact, my objective is the opposite one of attempting to 'rescue' what could be considered traditional human geography.

The essence of human geography is the study of the human settlement and occupancy of the earth. This has been one of the oldest themes of geography from the time of Strabo. The theme of human settlement and occupance has been defined in a variety of ways. The idea of landscape, forms of life, man–land relationships and geographical regions all embody something of this theme. In this work I have sought to incorporate some of these concepts about human geography in the phrase 'human activity on the land'. None of these short phrases in themselves is entirely adequate, but the need of a precise definition is not crucial, if the basic intent is clear (as I think it is). This traditional concept of human geography provided a challenge and a model for many geographers. Yet, although the aim was clear enough, the results of geographical analysis were often disappointing.

There is a history of concern among human geographers about the value and intellectual depth of their subject. This concern about the intellectual value of human geography has led geographers to make periodic re-appraisals of aims and objectives of their field. In these re-appraisals geographers have questioned not only the methods used but the subject matter itself. In a sense human geography has, on more than one occasion, been abandoned because geographers have been uncertain about the value of their contribution to knowledge. These redefinitions of human geography have created considerable confusion within and outside the discipline.

Yet, in seeking to establish a human geography that is more widely accepted within the academic world, geographers have allowed their philosophy to dictate their interests. Environmental determinism was an attempt to create a truly scientific discipline. It was based on the assumption that there was a causal connection between environment and society. This premise permitted the emergence of a vigorous theoretical geography, and geographers were able to claim their work as 'scientific'. Yet the progress of this theoretical geography was quite illusory, because the elementary procedures of scientific verification were not observed. As it became clear that the environmental theory was not well substantiated, human geographers recognized that their discipline could not be based on the investigation of a causal relationship whose validity was in doubt.

In the aftermath of environmentalism geographers became disillusioned with theory and turned towards empirical studies. The empirical approach was carried on within a philosophy of science which emphasized classification and enumeration as first steps towards the formulation of laws. The theoretical approach was not condemned because it was inappropriate but because it was premature. It was widely felt that geographers had, in adopting environmental determinism, attempted to jump over several steps in the scientific process. The empirical approach to regional geography it was hoped would provide a foundation for a more securely-based scientific geography. Yet, after many years of effort, it became increasingly clear that geographers were producing work in which description overshadowed analysis.

This was the climate of the 1950s out of which the new spatial geography emerged. In essence spatial geography was an attempt to breathe new life into the scientific approach by looking at spatial patterns using the new computer technology. The success of spatial geography as an applied discipline ensured its popularity. Yet as a foundation for a more scientific geography it was deficient. The laws and theories it needed were not developed on foundations that were any more secure than those on which environmentalism rested. Worse still, it was by no means clear that geographers were really getting at important questions with their new arsenal of social-scientific techniques.

The adoption of a spatial point of view failed to solve the fundamental problems of human geography. Although space is a consideration of importance in geography, it provides an inadequate definition of the field. Every discipline has an interest in space and time. A geography defined as a spatial discipline makes – as Hartshorne recognized – a dynamic historical geography logically impossible, and fails to provide geographers with a distinctive subject matter or point of view.

The basic problem of geography has been less a problem of traditional subject matter than a lack of an appropriate philosophy for geographical study. If one accepts the traditional idea that human geography is concerned with people and the landscapes they inhabit, one also accepts that geography is fundamentally an idiographic discipline. This is not because there are not parallels to be drawn between different areas and places, but rather because the essential question of geography is: 'Why do these people in this (particular) place differ from others?' The interest in human geography arises out of the differences among the peoples of the earth. Uniqueness is at the heart of geography.

Yet there are degrees of difference if not of uniqueness. Africa is unique. This statement can be made without fear of contradiction, but whether a particular Kenyan village is unique in the same sense is not quite so clear. Here its similarities to other villages might be more noticeable than its differences. In geography uniqueness is essentially a regional matter, a matter of scale. In a study of a large area the gross differences will be noticed, but as the scale becomes larger the kinds of differences noticed will become more subtle, but it is axiomatic that the peoples of no two areas will have identical characteristics.

If one takes it as given that human activity is not uniform over the earth, and that important differences exist between places such as Texas, northeastern Brazil and Thailand, how can a study of such differences be made intellectually rewarding? It is at this point that geographers have had to deal with the most serious criticisms. Critics of regional approaches to geography have pointed out that a geographer draws upon the work of such specialists as the geologist, botanist and economist, but does not make a distinctive contribution of his own. Such criticisms, far from being unjustified, have often been fully deserved. There has been a tendency for geographers to treat human activity as a spectacle. The crops people grew and the locations of their towns were seen as the results of climate, soils or fordable streams. In more modern work distance was treated as the dominant geographical factor and elaborate models of spatial interaction were developed. The spatial approach, however, failed to provide much insight into regional distinctiveness.

A concern with regional distinctiveness is at the same time a concern with historical geography. If regional approaches have failed it is largely because this central need for a historical perspective has been ignored. The various peoples of the world have been created by different historical experiences, and these experiences account for the variety of world cultures. In seeking to provide insight into the culture of a people or peoples, the geographer must probe its historical roots. A good regional geographer must also be a good historical geographer. For example, modern problems of development in Africa must be seen in the context of colonialism and its aftermath. Modern South Africa cannot be understood unless there is some appreciation of the historical forces that have created it.

Historical geography is a field in its own right, but it is also the foundation of regional geography. In regional geography the present provides the terminal point of what should ideally be a historical analysis of an area from its earliest beginnings as a 'home of man'. In practice, in a regional geography, the extent of historical analysis will be a function of the scale and purpose of the study. It is, however, essential that human activities of a region be understood in terms of their changing internal relationships. If human geographers can provide a regional perspective on the world and its problems (as these problems are defined in a historical geographical context), they can make a distinctive contribution to knowledge.

A historical approach to regional geography provides an alternative way of looking at the human settlement and occupancy of the earth. It is true to the traditions of geography. The approach is grounded in empirical analysis, but it is designed to avoid the overemphasis on description that did so much to destroy interest in traditional regional geography. The approach emphasizes that geographers can provide a distinctive perspective on the people of the earth by treating human forms of life as expressions of historical experience. It is by cultivating our own distinctive geographical point of view that human and historical geographers can make their most valuable contribution to scholarship.

Select bibliography of philosophical and methodological topics

Althusser, L. *For Marx* (London, Allen Lane, 1969).

Althusser, L. 'and Balibar, E. *Reading Capital* (New York, Pantheon Books, 1970).

Baker, A. R. H. 'Rethinking historical geography' in A. R. H. Baker (ed.), *Progress in historical geography* (Newton Abbot, David and Charles, 1972), pp. 11–28.

Baker, A. R. H. 'Historical geography: a new beginning?' *Progress in Human Geography*, **4** (1979), 560–70.

Bergin, T. G. and Fisch, M. H. (eds.), *The new science of Giambattista Vico* (New York, Anchor Books, 1961).

Billinge, M. 'In search of negativism: phenomenology and historical geography', *Journal of Historical Geography*, **3** (1977), 55–67.

Bowden, M. J. in *Economic Geography*, **46** (1970), 202–3.

Carr, E. H. *What is history?* (Harmondsworth, Penguin Books, 1964).

Clark, A. H. *The invasion of New Zealand by peoples, plants and animals* (New Brunswick, N.J., Rutgers University Press, 1949).

Clark, A. H. 'Historical geography' in P. E. James and C. P. Jones (eds.), *American geography: inventory and prospect* (Syracuse, Syracuse University Press for the Society of American Geographers, 1954), pp. 70–105.

Clark, A. H. *Three centuries and the island* (Toronto, University of Toronto Press, 1959).

Clark A.H. 'Geographic change: a theme for economic history', *Journal of Economic History*, **20** (1960), 607–16.

Clark, A. H. 'Historical geography in North America', in A. R. H. Baker (ed.), *Progress in historical geography* (Newton Abbot, David and Charles, 1972), pp. 129–43.

Collingwood, R. G. and Myers, J. N. L. *Roman Britain and the English settlements* (London, Oxford University Press, 1937).

Collingwood, R. G. *An autobiography* (Oxford, Oxford University Press, 1939).

Collingwood, R. G. *The idea of history* (New York, Oxford University Press, 1956; first published, 1946).

Darby, H. C. 'On the relations of geography and history', *Transactions and Papers of the Institute of British Geographers*, **19** (1953), 1–11.

Darby, H. C. 'Historical geography', in H. P. R. Finberg (ed.), *Approaches to history* (Toronto, University of Toronto Press, 1962), pp. 127–56.

Darby, H. C. *Domesday England* (Cambridge, Cambridge University Press, 1977).

De Koninck, R. 'Le matérialisme historique en géographie', *Cahiers de Géographie du Québec*, **22** (1978), 117–22.

Dray, W. *Laws and explanation in history* (Oxford, Oxford University Press, 1957).

Dray, W. (ed.), *Philosophical analysis and history* (New York, Harper and Row, 1966).

Ernst, J. A. and Merrens, H. R. 'Praxis and theory in the writing of American historical geography', *Journal of Historical Geography*, **4** (1978), 277–90.

Foster, R. and Ranum, O. (eds.), *Family and society: selections from the Annales, economies, sociétés, civilisations* (Baltimore, The Johns Hopkins University Press, 1976).

Gardiner, P. (ed.), *Theories of history* (Glencoe, The Free Press, 1959).

Glacken, C. J. *Traces on the Rhodian shore: nature and culture in Western thought from ancient times to the end of the eighteenth century* (Berkeley, University of California Press, 1967).

Goldstein, L. G., 'Collingwood's theory of historical knowing', *History and Theory*, **9** (1970), 3–36.

Gregory, D. 'Rethinking historical geography', *Area*, **8** (1976), 295–8.

Gregory, D. 'The discourse of the past: phenomenology, structuralism and historical geography', *Journal of Historical Geography*, **4** (1978), 161–73.

Gregory, D. 'Social change and spatial structures' in T. Carlstein, D. Parkes and N. Thrift (eds.), *Making sense of time*, vol. 1 (London, Edward Arnold, 1978), pp. 38–46.

Gregory, D. *Ideology, science and human geography* (London, Hutchinson, 1978).

Guelke, L. 'Problems of scientific explanation in geography', *The Canadian Geographer*, **15** (1971), 38–53.

Guelke, L. 'An idealist alternative in human geography, *Annals of the Association of American Geographers*, **64** (1974), 193–202.

Harris, R. C. 'Theory and synthesis in historical geography', *The Canadian Geographer*, **15** (1971), 157–72.

Harris, R. C. 'The historical mind and the practice of geography' in D. Ley and M. Samuels (ed.), *Humanistic geography: problems and prospects* (Chicago, Maroufa Press, 1978), pp. 123–37.

Harrison, R. T. and Livingstone, D. N. 'There and back again – towards a critique of idealist human geography', *Area*, **11** (1979), 75–8.

Hartshorne, R. *The nature of geography* (Lancaster, Pa., Association of American Geographers, 1939).

Hartshorne, R. *Perspective on the nature of geography* (Chicago, Rand McNally for the Association of American Geographers, 1959).

Harvey, D. *Explanation in geography* (London, Edward Arnold, 1969).

Harvey, D. *Social justice and the city* (London, Edward Arnold, 1973).

Hempel, C. 'The function of general laws in history', in P. Gardiner (ed.), *Theories of history* (Glencoe, The Free Press, 1959).

Hempel, C. *Aspects of scientific explanation* (New York, The Free Press, 1965).

Hempel, C. *Philosophy of natural science* (Englewood Cliffs, N.J., Prentice-Hall, 1966).

Kirk, W. 'Historical geography and the concept of the behavioural environment', *Indian Geographical Journal*, Silver Jubilee Volume (1952), 152–60.

Koelsch, W. A. in *Economic Geography*, **46** (1970), 201–2.

Lowenthal, D. and Bowden, M. J. (eds.), *Geographies of mind: essays in historical geography in honor of John Kirkland Wright* (New York, Oxford University Press, 1976).

Lowther, G. R. 'Idealist history and historical geography', *The Canadian Geographer*, **14** (1959), 31–6.

Meinig, D. W. 'Prologue: Andrew Hill Clark, historical geographer', in J. R. Gibson (ed.), *European settlement and development in North America: essays on geographical change in honour and memory of Andrew Hill Clark* (Toronto, University of Toronto Press, 1978).

Mink, L. O. *Mind, history and dialectic: the philosophy of R. G. Collingwood* (Bloomington, Indiana University Press, 1969).

Moodie, D. W. and Lehr, J. C. 'Fact and theory in historical geography', *The Professional Geographer*, **18** (1976), 132–5.

Nagel, E. 'Determinism in history', in W. Dray (ed.), *Philosophical analysis and history* (New York, Harper and Row, 1966).

Oakeshott, M. *Experience and its modes* (Cambridge, Cambridge University Press, 1933).

Popper, K. *Conjectures and refutations*, 2nd edn (New York, Basic Books, 1965).

Prince, H. C. 'Real, imagined and abstract worlds of the past', *Progress in Geography*, **3** (1971), 1–86.

Prince, H. C. 'Historical geography in 1980' in E. H. Brown (ed.), *Geography yesterday and tomorrow* (Oxford, Oxford University Press, 1980), pp. 229–50.

Rubinoff, L. *Collingwood and the reform of metaphysics* (Toronto, University of Toronto Press, 1970).

Sauer, C. O. 'Foreword to historical geography', *Annals of the Association of American Geographers*, **31** (1941), 1–24.

Taylor, G. (ed.), *Geography in the twentieth century*, 3rd edn (London, Methuen, 1957).

Thompson, E. P. *The making of the English working class* (Harmondsworth, Penguin Books, 1968; first published, 1963).

Thompson, E. P. *The poverty of theory and other essays* (New York and London, Monthly Review Press, 1978).

Tuan, Y. F. *The hydrological cycle and the wisdom of God: a theme in geoteleology* (Toronto, University of Toronto Press, 1967).

Watts, S. J. and Watts, S. J. 'On the idealist alternative in geography and history', *The Professional Geographer*, **30** (1978), 123–27.

Wright, J. K. 'Terrae incognitae: the place of imagination in geography', *Annals of the Association of American Geographers*, **37** (1947), 1–15. Reprinted in J. K. Wright *Human nature in geography* (Cambridge, Mass., Harvard University Press, 1966), pp. 68–88.

Wynn, G. 'W. F. Ganong, A. H. Clark and the historical geography of Maritime Canada', *Acadiensis*, **10** (1981), 3–28.

Index

historical geography, as analysis of geographical processes, 9
historical geography, as foundation of regional geography, 101–2
historical geography, as an interdisciplinary field, 11
historical geography, as a spectacle, 10
historical geography, definition of, 3–4
historical geography, differentiated from history, 7–8, 47–8
historical inference, 2
historical knowledge, 1, 3, 16, 34, 45
historical materialism, 61–6
historical materialism, as a philosophy, 63
historical materialism, 'weak' formulation, 61–2
historical meaning, *see* meaning, historical
historical meaning, criterion of, 46, 52, 59
historical narrative, 15, 19
historical process, 12, 14, 17, 18
historical scepticism, 52
historical scholar, essential task of,
historical scholar, privileged position of, 2
historical significance, 1, 5, 15, 20, 45–6, 51, 53
historical understanding, as elucidation of meaning, 41–2, 45
historical understanding, in geography, 2–3
historical understanding, as re-enactment of thought, 2
historicity, criterion of, 18, 53
history, as an autonomous field of knowledge, 1, 21
history, as elucidation of meaning, 66–7, 68
history, as a full account of change, 18
history, as a law-applying science, 58
history, differentiated from geography, 7–8
history, discipline of, 11, 12, 14
history, natural-scientific concept of, 53
history, not a synonym for the past, 3, 5
history, temporal concept of, 6, 8–12, 15–16, 21
history, 'total', 13
human activity, as reflection of mind, 3
human geography, definition of, 3, 99–102
human settlement, 102
'humanistic' geography, 14, 15, 21
hypotheses, ad-hoc, 28, 63

idealism, 16–18, 99
idealism, philosophy of, 2, 53
ideologies, 61, 64
institutions, 18, 27
interdisciplinary study, 13
irrational, 38–9, 44

judgement, in history, 15–16
judgement, subjectivity in, 15–16

Kant, I., 6–7
knowledge, geographers contribution to, 99

landscape, 99
landscape, *see* cultural landscape
laws, 9, 17–18, 41
law, confirmation and acceptance of, 57
laws, criteria of universality, 55–9
laws, probabilistic, 57–9
laws, role in objective explanation, 49
laws, in scientific explanation, 57–9
Lehr, J. C., 17
Lösch, 60

Marx, as foundation of theoretical history, 62–3
Marxism, original formulation, 62
Marxism, structuralist interpretation, 63
Marxist approaches, 61–6
meaning, historical, 16, 26, 41–2, 44–6, 48, 51–2
Merrens, H. R., 76
mind, independence of, 1
mind, theory of, 49
mind, subconscious, 44–5
Mink, L. O., 42–3
models, in historical geography, 13
models, role in explanation, 59–60
quantitative analysis, 67
question and answer, 48–9
questions, in historical enquiry, 48–9

rational action, 38
rational understanding, 29–34
rational thought, nature of, 26–9
re-enactment, *see* re-thinking
real, the, 17
regional geography, 101–2
re-thinking, 46–7, 48–50, 53
re-thinking, as foundation of historical fields, 2
re-thinking, as imaginative understanding, 30, 39–40

Sauer, C. O., 6, 8, 10, 21, 48
scale of enquiry, 67, 102
science, use of results in historical enquiry, 43
scientific approach, in historical geography, 13
scientific explanation, 55
sciences, law-applying, 56–7
scientific methods, 66–8
scientific procedures, in study of natural world, 1
selection, *see* facts, selection of
significance, criterion of in historical geography, 3
social sciences, 1, 13–14, 43, 61
social science, undeveloped state of, 58
social theory, 28–9, 43

L. I. H. E.
THE MARKLAND LIBRARY
STAND PARK RD., LIVERPOOL, L16 9JD

L.H.E.
THE MARKLAND LIBRARY
STAND PARK RD., LIVERPOOL, L16 9JD